# Nancy Lindop's Genealogies
# Volume 1

## Lindop Family Charts

by
Nancy and Geoffrey Lindop

Cover Picture:
George Edwin Lindop of College Fields, Woore (1868-1913),
who was Geoffrey's grandfather. In the background is Lindop
Wood in Derbyshire taken in 2004.

*First published 2014*
*Revised 2015*

Published by:
Mercianotes
Wigton
CA7 5AQ
United Kingdom

© 2015 Mercianotes

ISBN: 978-1-905999-21-7

# Examples of symbols used in the book

Position on this chart 8/2/9

Row D column a    Row D column b

Position on this chart

Row A column a    Row A column b

Position on this chart

Row A column c    Row A column d

Surnames are in uppercase

ID Number

'=' symbol for married

Don't know when Isaac was born but probably 1881-1889 by reference to his marriage. If we only knew when he died 'D' would replace the 'M'

If this line were dotted it would signify that Mary Ann's parents are unknown but probably Isaac and Elizabeth

Mary Ann GILBERT was born before 1835 and died after 1871. She was probably born 1820-1829 (Hence 'B' in the ID)

Phoebe Ann SHAW (person b) married John LINDOP in 1870. Her second marriage (denoted by b2) was to James PAGE

**Family tree**

8.2.9Da
William LINDOP = Mary SILVESTER 8.2.9Db
(1785-1848) (1783-1878)
785139 783168

Ac Isaac GILBERT 8JMI173
Ad Elizabeth 8JMI174

Bg Edwin LINDOP (1831-1874) 831492 = Bh Mary Ann GILBERT <1835-1871> **High Office** 82B493

Bc James PAGE <1813-1828> 85M315 = b2 Bb Phoebe Ann SHAW (1856-1927) 85B314

b1 = 1870
9.3.1Be John LINDOP (1845-1886) 845313

9.4.1Ba Elizabeth
9.4.2Bb Thomas Silvester
9.4/1Bc William
9.4.3Bd John
9.4.4Bc George
9.4.1Bf Mary Elizabeth

→ Chipnal, near Cheswardine

**Birmingham**

Ca Vernon LINDOP (1871-1939) 871418
Cb Leila Elizabeth LINDOP (1873- ) 873419
Cc Crompton LINDOP (1874-1901) 874420
Cd Marshal LINDOP (1876-1948) 876421
Ce Marguerite Dora LINDOP (1879-1891) 879423
Cf Repton LINDOP (1880-1938) 880524
Cg Harold LINDOP (1871-1939) 871525

William LINDOP
Born 1785
Died 1848
ID: 785139

His children all born at Chipnal. If he had moved to another place a second location would be in bold. On this line above the name of the first person to be born in that place.

**ID Numbers**

First three digits are the year of birth (omitting the leading '1') followed by a unique 3 or 4 digit number. If underlined it signifys the person had no children.

[ born in the year
( baptised in the year
< born before

] died in the year
) buried in the year
> died after the year

# Part 1

# Early History

Aa
Henry DE LEYIS
*205028*

**Carlton**

| Ba | Bb | Bc | Bd |
|---|---|---|---|
| Richard DE LEYIS | Thomas DE LEYIS | Robert DE LEYIS | Walther DE LEYIS |
| *22B181* | *22B182* | alias | *22B183* |
| | | Robert DE LYNDOP | |
| | | *235087* | |

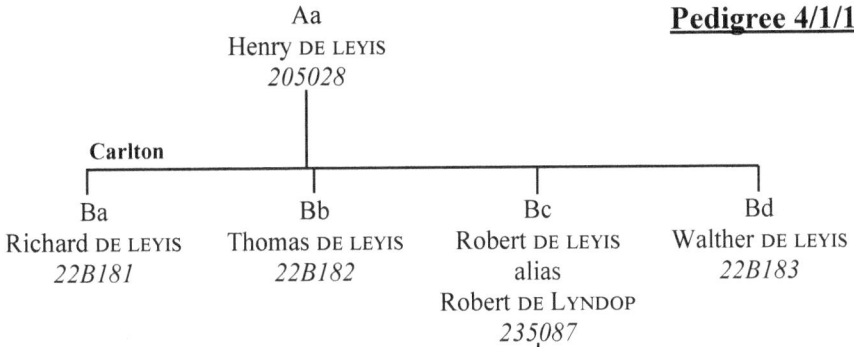

*Know ye that I Robert de Lyndop, son of Henry de Lechis have conceded given to John my son for his homage and service all those lands and tenements which I had of Henry son of Richard Bargayn of Midleton in exchange for all those lands which I formerly had in the territory of Lyndop and a piece of meadow called Brodemedere in Wynstanley in the field of Little Roylewley with the appurts. of the yearly rent of one penny at Xmas with due service to the lord of the fee. Warranty and witness Adam lord of Roulesley, John his son; Robert Bozon of Edenshor; Thomas de Beyel; Will de Candal; Robert de Stanton; Will Ffremon of Great Rowlesley and other.*

*Haddon Hall mss No.213
transcribed by the Rev. Kerry,
it is dated the middle of the
13th century.*

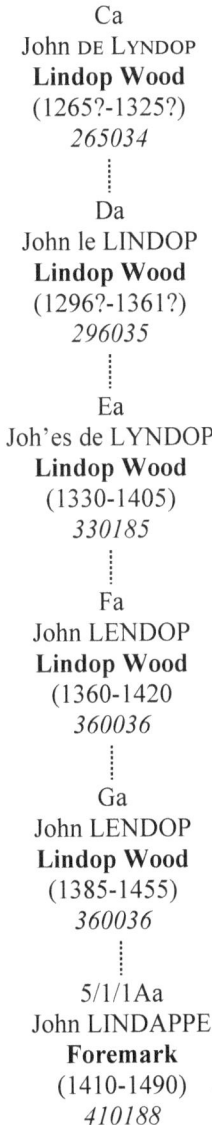

Ca
John DE LYNDOP
**Lindop Wood**
(1265?-1325?)
*265034*

⋮

Da
John le LINDOP
**Lindop Wood**
(1296?-1361?)
*296035*

⋮

Ea
Joh'es de LYNDOP
**Lindop Wood**
(1330-1405)
*330185*

⋮

Fa
John LENDOP
**Lindop Wood**
(1360-1420
*360036*

⋮

Ga
John LENDOP
**Lindop Wood**
(1385-1455)
*360036*

⋮

5/1/1Aa
John LINDAPPE
**Foremark**
(1410-1490)
*410188*

This chart is discussed in more detail in *Lindop: A Family History* by John Barford Lindop published by Mercianotes. ISBN: 9781522882947

# Pedigree 5/1/1

This chart is discussed in more detail in *Lindop: A Family History* by John Barford Lindop published by Mercianotes. (ISBN: 9781522882947 )

**Chesterfield**

**Alderwasley**

**Rowsley - Bakewell Area**

**Foremark**

4/1/1Ha
John LINDAPPE
Of **Foremark**
(1410-1490)
*410188*

Ba
Nicholas LYNDOPPE
of **Derby**
(1440-1510)
*440190*

Ca
Nicholas LINDOP
(1453-1499)
*453068*

Cb
Robert WYNFELD
of Matlock
*45M1399*

Cc
William LINDOP
(1453-1499)
*453124*

Da
Thomas LINDOP
(1483-1538)
*483109*

1508

Db
Matilda WYNFELD
*48M177*

Dc
Roger LINDOP
(1480-1542)
*480098*

Dd
Alice
*48M1082*

Df
John LINDOP
(1480-1536)
*480037*

Dg
Helen
*48M178*

Ea
Thomas
LYNDCHOP
*52R111*

Eb
Philip
LYNDOPP
*53R070*

6/1/1Aa
John
LINDOP
(1500-1557)
*500040*

6/2/1Ba
John
LINDOP
*507039*

6/2/1Bb
Alice
LENDOPPE
*50B196*

6/3/1Aa
Thomas
LINDOP
*505110*

6/3/1Ac
Elizabeth
LINDOP
*506013*

6/3/1Ad
John
LINDOP
*507038*

# Pedigree 6/1/1

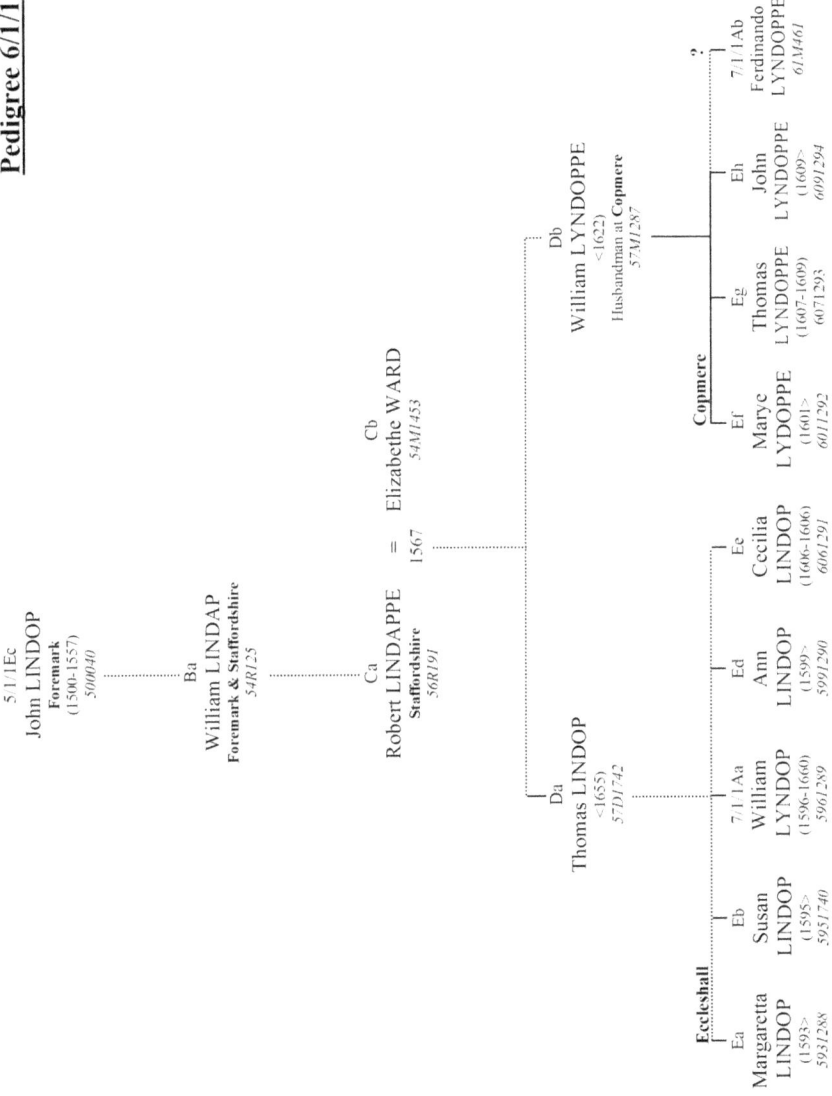

**5/1/1Ec**
John LINDOP
**Foremark**
(1500-1557)
*50/040*

**Ba**
William LINDAP
**Foremark & Staffordshire**
*54R125*

**Ca**
Robert LINDAPPE
**Staffordshire**
*56R191*

**Cb**
Elizabethe WARD
*54M1453*

= 1567

**Da**
Thomas LINDOP
<1655>
*57D1742*

**Db**
William LYNDOPPE
<1622>
Husbandman at **Copmere**
*57M1287*

**Eccleshall**

**Ea**
Margaretta
LINDOP
(1593>
*593/288*

**Eb**
Susan
LINDOP
(1595>
*595/740*

**7/1/1Aa**
William
LYNDOP
(1596-1660)
*596/289*

**Ed**
Ann
LINDOP
(1599>
*599/290*

**Ee**
Cecilia
LINDOP
(1606-1606)
*606/291*

**Copmere**

**Ef**
Marye
LYNDOPPE
(1601>
*601/292*

**Eg**
Thomas
LYNDOPPE
(1607-1609)
*607/293*

**Eh**
John
LYNDOPPE
(1609>
*609/294*

**?**

**7/1/1Ab**
Ferdinando
LYNDOPPE
*61M461*

**Pedigree 6/2/1**

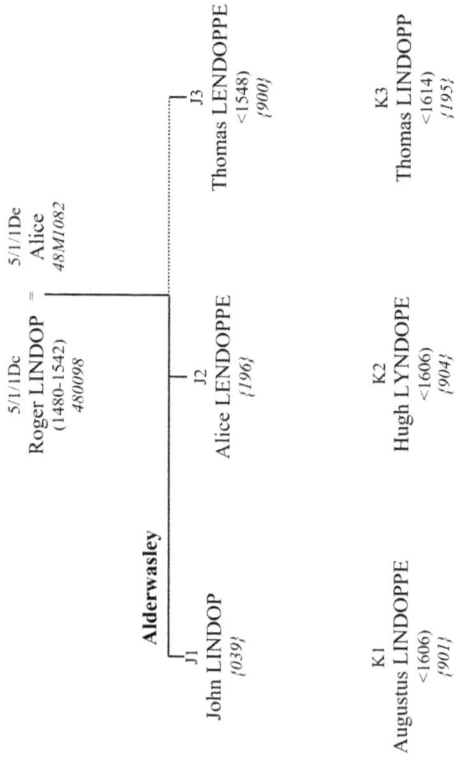

**Alderwasley**

J1
John LINDOP
*{039}*

5/1/1Dc
Roger LINDOP
(1480-1542)
*480098*

= 5/1/1De
Alice
*48M1082*

J2
Alice LENDOPPE
*{196}*

J3
Thomas LENDOPPE
<1548)
*{900}*

K1
Augustus LINDOPPE
<1606)
*{901}*

K2
Hugh LYNDOPE
<1606)
*{904}*

K3
Thomas LINDOPP
<1614)
*{195}*

K4
Anne LYNDOPE
<1622)
*{903}*

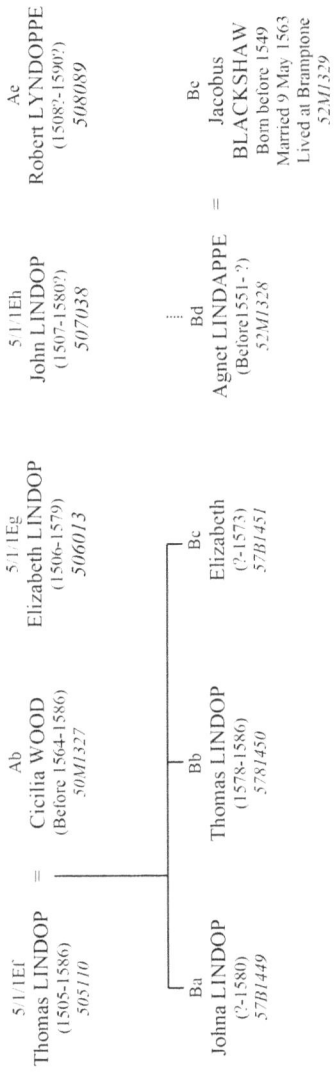

Ae
Robert LYNDOPPE
(1508?-1590?)
*508089*

5.1.1Eh
John LINDOP
(1507-1580?)
*507038*

5.1.1Eg
Elizabeth LINDOP
(1506-1579)
*506013*

Ab
Cicilia WOOD
(Before 1564-1586)
*50M1327*

=

5.1.1Ef
Thomas LINDOP
(1505-1586)
*505110*

Bc
Elizabeth
(?-1573)
*57B1451*

Bb
Thomas LINDOP
(1578-1586)
*57B1450*

Ba
Johna LINDOP
(?-1580)
*57B1449*

Bd
Agnet LINDAPPE
(Before 1551-?)
*52M1328*

=

Bc
Jacobus
BLACKSHAW
Born before 1549
Married 9 May 1563
Lived at Bramptone
*52M1329*

**Pedigree 6/3/1**

**Chesterfield**

5/1/1Ea
Thomas
LYNDCHOP
*52R111*

5/1/1Eb
Philip
LYNDOPP
*53R070*

Ac
Robert
LYNDOPE
<1563)
*49D199*

=

Ad
Isabel
*50M200*

**Birstall**

Ba
Jone
LYNDOPE
*52M1458*

Bb
Elizabeth
LYNDOPE
<1575)
*52M203*

Bc
Alice
LYNDOPE
*52M1460*

She had 3
daughters

Bd
Agnes
LYNOPE
*52M1461*

Bc
Margaret
LYNDOPE
*52M1463*

Bf
Isabel
LYNDOPE
*52M1462*

Bg
Baladon
LYNDOPE
A boy
*52M1464*

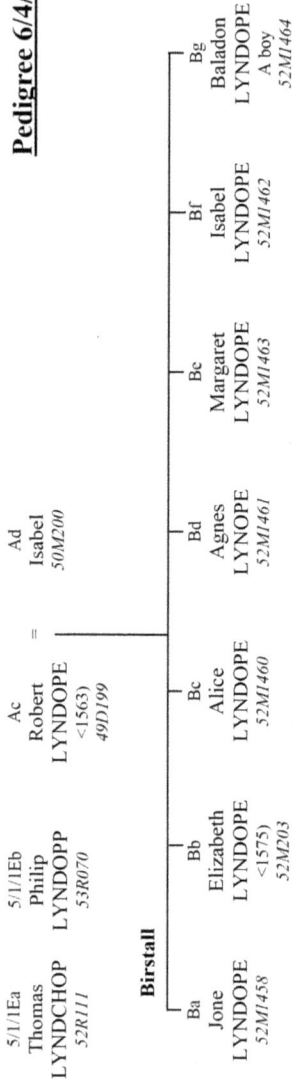

Ca
Hugh LYNDOP
died 1614 in
**Sheffield**
*54D202*

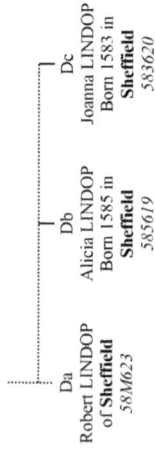

Da
Robert LINDOP
of **Sheffield**
*58M623*

Db
Alicia LINDOP
Born 1585 in
**Sheffield**
*585619*

Dc
Joanna LINDOP
Born 1583 in
**Sheffield**
*583620*

Dd
Em LINDOP
Of **Repton**
*58M021*

Ea
Dorothea LINDOP
Born: 1609 in
**Sheffield**
*609624*

5/1/1Ea
Thomas
LYNDCHOP
**Rowsley**
*52R111*

5/1/1Eb
Philip
LYNDOPP
**Bakewell**
*53R070*

5/1/1Ec
John
LINDOP
**Foremark**
(1500-1557)
*50I040*

5/1/1Ed
John
LINDOP
**Alderwasley**
*507039*

5/1/1Ef
Thomas
LINDOP
**Chesterfield**
*505110*

5/1/1Eh
John
LINDOP
**Chesterfield**
*507038*

Ba
Richard LINDOP
<1573>
**Wybunbury**
*50D209*

Ca
Robertus LINDOP   =   1571
Married 1571 in
**Wybunbury**
*55M090*

Cb
Anna PARRAT
<1559-1580>
**Wybunbury**
*55M163*

See chart 6/5/4 3 sons and 3 daughters

Bb
Robte LINDOP   =   1540
<1526-1559>
**Wybunbury**
*510728*

Bc
Margaret
<1528-1559>
**Wybunbury**
*51M204*

Cc
Robert
LINDOP
(1553-1612)
**Wybunbury**
*553256*

Cd
Richard
LINDOP
**Wybunbury**
*55M1525*

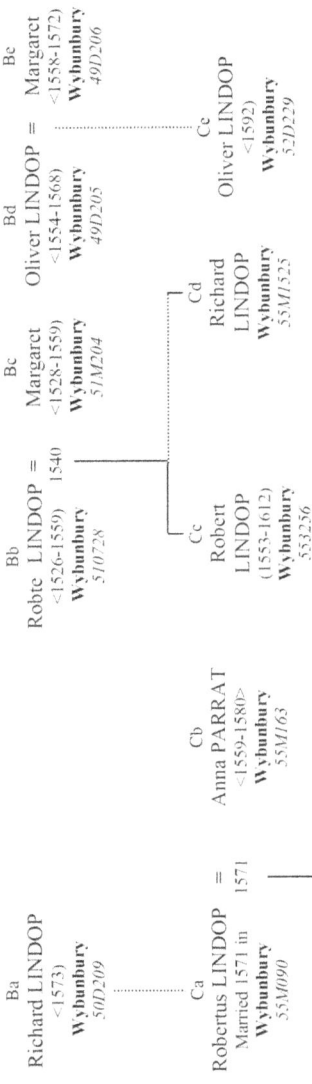

See chart 6/5/6 4 sons and 4 daughters

Bd
Oliver LINDOP   =
<1554-1568>
**Wybunbury**
*49D205*

Bc
Margaret
<1558-1572>
**Wybunbury**
*49D206*

Cc
Oliver LINDOP
<1592>
**Wybunbury**
*52D229*

# Pedigree 6/5/2

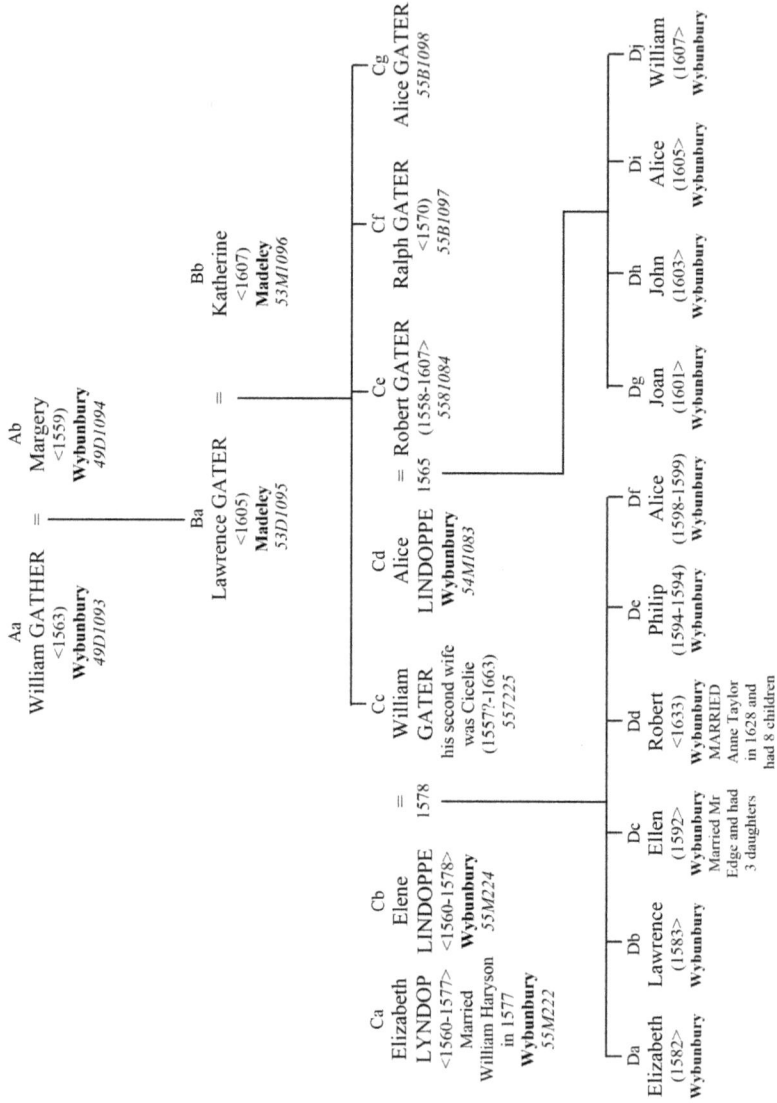

Aa
William GATHER
<1563>
**Wybunbury**
*49D1093*

=

Ab
Margery
<1559>
**Wybunbury**
*49D1094*

Ba
Lawrence GATER
<1605>
**Madeley**
*53D1095*

=

Bb
Katherine
<1607>
**Madeley**
*53M1096*

Ca
Elizabeth
LYNDOP
<1560-1577>
Married
William Haryson
in 1577
**Wybunbury**
*55M222*

Cb
Elene
LINDOPPE
<1560-1578>
**Wybunbury**
*55M224*

=  1578

Cc
William
GATER
his second wife
was Cicelie
(1557?-1663)
*557225*

Cd
Alice
LINDOPPE
**Wybunbury**
*54M1083*

=  1565

Ce
Robert GATER
(1558-1607>
*55B1084*

=

Cf
Ralph GATER
<1570>
*55B1097*

Cg
Alice GATER
*55B1098*

Da
Elizabeth
(1582)
**Wybunbury**

Db
Lawrence
(1583)
**Wybunbury**

Dc
Ellen
(1592)
**Wybunbury**
Married Mr
Edge and had
3 daughters

Dd
Robert
<1633>
**Wybunbury**
MARRIED
Anne Taylor
in 1628 and
had 8 children

De
Philip
(1594-1594)
**Wybunbury**

Df
Alice
(1598-1599)
**Wybunbury**

Dg
Joan
(1601>
**Wybunbury**

Dh
John
(1603>
**Wybunbury**

Di
Alice
(1605>
**Wybunbury**

Dj
William
(1607>
**Wybunbury**

# Pedigree 6/5/3

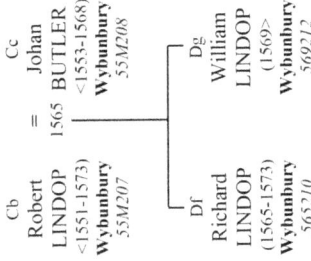

Cb
Robert
LINDOP
<1551-1573)
**Wybunbury**
*55M207*

= 1565

Cc
Johan
BUTLER
<1553-1568)
**Wybunbury**
*55M208*

Df
Richard
LINDOP
(1565-1573)
**Wybunbury**
*565210*

Dg
William
LINDOP
(1569)
**Wybunbury**
*569212*

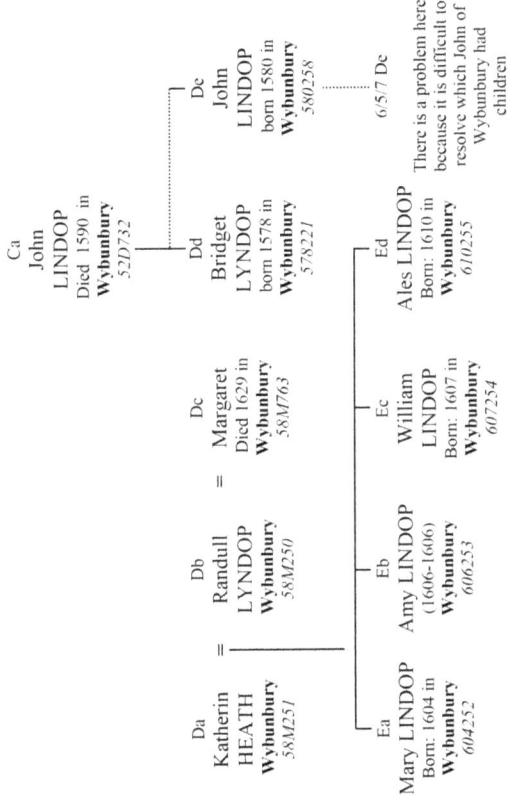

Ca
John
LINDOP
Died 1590 in
**Wybunbury**
*52D732*

Dd
Bridget
LYNDOP
born 1578 in
**Wybunbury**
*578227*

De
John
LINDOP
born 1580 in
**Wybunbury**
*580258*

6/5/7 De

There is a problem here
because it is difficult to
resolve which John of
Wybunbury had
children

Da
Katherin
HEATH
**Wybunbury**
*58M251*

=

Db
Randull
LYNDOP
**Wybunbury**
*58M250*

=

Dc
Margaret
Died 1629 in
**Wybunbury**
*58M763*

Ea
Mary LINDOP
Born: 1604 in
**Wybunbury**
*604252*

Eb
Amy LINDOP
(1606-1606)
**Wybunbury**
*606253*

Ec
William
LINDOP
Born: 1607 in
**Wybunbury**
*607254*

Ed
Ales LINDOP
Born: 1610 in
**Wybunbury**
*610255*

**Pedigree 6/5/4**

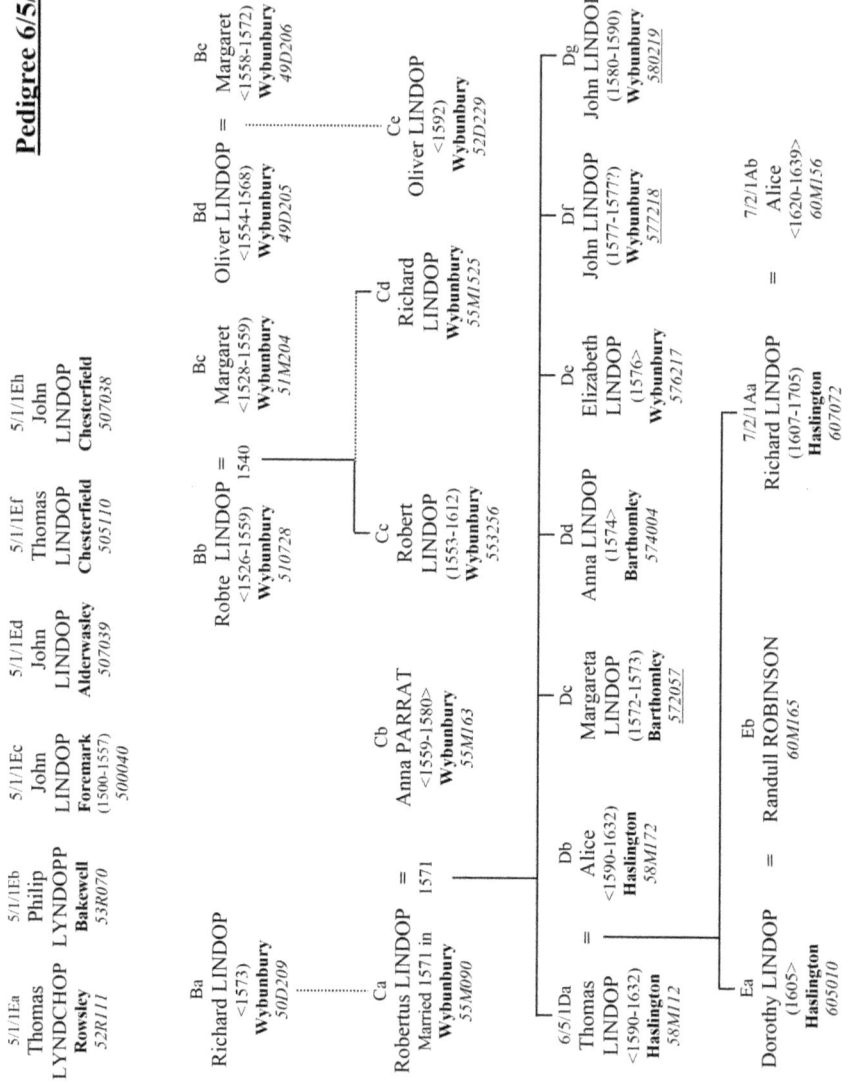

5/1/1Ea
Thomas
LYNDCHOP
**Rowsley**
*52R111*

5/1/1Eb
Philip
LYNDOPP
**Bakewell**
*53R070*

5/1/1Ec
John
LINDOP
**Foremark**
(1500-1557)
*500040*

5/1/1Ed
John
LINDOP
**Alderwasley**
*507039*

5/1/1Ef
Thomas
LINDOP
**Chesterfield**
*505110*

5/1/1Eh
John
LINDOP
**Chesterfield**
*507038*

Be
Margaret
<1558-1572>
**Wybunbury**
*49D206*

Ba
Richard LINDOP
<1573>
**Wybunbury**
*50D209*

Bb
Robte LINDOP  =  1540
<1526-1559>
**Wybunbury**
*510728*

Bc
Margaret
<1528-1559>
**Wybunbury**
*51M204*

Bd
Oliver LINDOP  =
<1554-1568>
**Wybunbury**
*49D205*

Cb
Anna PARRAT
<1559-1580>
**Wybunbury**
*55M163*

Ca
Robertus LINDOP  =  1571
Married 1571 in
**Wybunbury**
*55M090*

Cc
Robert
LINDOP
(1553-1612)
**Wybunbury**
*553256*

Cd
Richard
LINDOP
**Wybunbury**
*55M1525*

Ce
Oliver LINDOP
<1592>
**Wybunbury**
*52D229*

Db
Alice
<1590-1632>
**Haslington**
*58M172*

Dc
Margareta
LINDOP
(1572-1573)
**Barthomley**
*572057*

Dd
Anna LINDOP
(1574>
**Barthomley**
*574004*

De
Elizabeth
LINDOP
(1576>
**Wybunbury**
*576217*

Df
John LINDOP
(1577-1577?)
**Wybunbury**
*577218*

Dg
John LINDOP
(1580-1590)
**Wybunbury**
*580219*

6/5/1Da
Thomas
LINDOP  =
<1590-1632)
**Haslington**
*58M112*

Ea
Dorothy LINDOP  =  Randull ROBINSON
(1605>
**Haslington**
*605010*

Eb
Randull ROBINSON
*60M165*

7/2/1Aa
Richard LINDOP
(1607-1705)
**Haslington**
*607072*

7/2/1Ab
Alice
<1620-1639>
*60M156*

# Pedigree 6/5/5

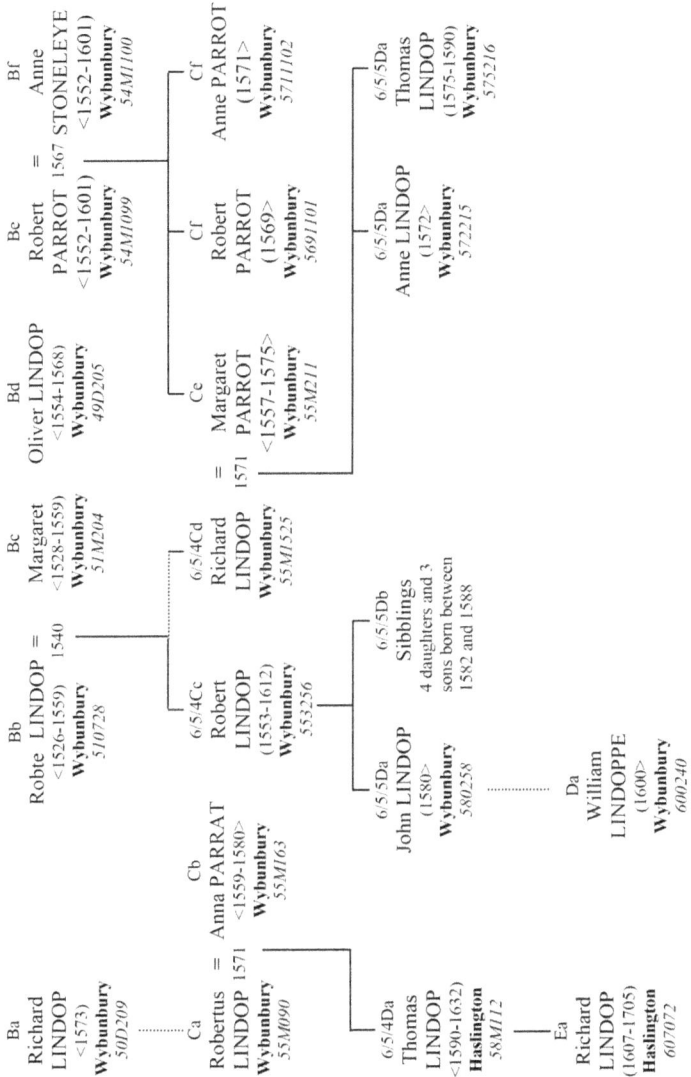

Ba
Richard
LINDOP
<1573>
**Wybunbury**
*50D209*

Ca
Robertus =  Anna PARRAT
LINDOP  1571  <1559-1580>
**Wybunbury**  **Wybunbury**
*55M090*  *55M163*

Cb

Bb
Robte  LINDOP  =  1540
<1526-1559>
**Wybunbury**
*510728*

Bc
Margaret
<1528-1559>
**Wybunbury**
*51M204*

6/5/4Cc
Robert
LINDOP
(1553-1612)
**Wybunbury**
*553256*

6/5/4Cd
Richard
LINDOP
*55M1525*

Bd
Oliver LINDOP
<1554-1568>
**Wybunbury**
*49D205*

Bc
Robert
PARROT  1567
<1552-1601)
**Wybunbury**
*54M1099*

=

Bf
Anne
STONELEYE
<1552-1601)
**Wybunbury**
*54M1100*

Ce
Margaret
PARROT
<1557-1575>
**Wybunbury**
*55M211*

=  1571

Cf
Robert
PARROT
(1569>
**Wybunbury**
*5691101*

Cf
Anne PARROT
(1571>
**Wybunbury**
*5711102*

6/5/5Db
Sibblings
4 daughters and 3
sons born between
1582 and 1588

6/5/5Da
John LINDOP
(1580>
**Wybunbury**
*580258*

Da
William
LINDOPPE
(1600>
**Wybunbury**
*600240*

6/5/4Da
Thomas
LINDOP
<1590-1632)
**Haslington**
*58M112*

Ea
Richard
LINDOP
(1607-1705)
**Haslington**
*607072*

6/5/5Da
Anne LINDOP
(1572>
**Wybunbury**
*572215*

6/5/5Da
Thomas
LINDOP
(1575-1590)
**Wybunbury**
*575216*

**Pedigree 6/5/6**

This chart is discussed in more detail in *Lindop: A Family History* by John Barford Lindop published by Mercianotes. (ISBN: 9781522882947 )

Ba
Richard
LINDOP
<1573)
**Wybunbury**
*50D209*

Ca
Robertus = Anna PARRAT
LINDOP 1571   <1559-1580>
**Wybunbury**   **Wybunbury**
*55M090*   *55M163*

Bb
Robte  LINDOP  =  1540
<1526-1559>
**Wybunbury**
*51D728*

Bc
Margaret
<1528-1559>
**Wybunbury**
*51M204*

Bd
Oliver LINDOP
<1554-1568>
**Wybunbury**
*49D205*

6/5/4Cc
Robert LINDOP
(1553-1612)
**Wybunbury**
*553256*

Cd
Agnes
<1565-1587>
**Wybunbury**
*55M257*

=  1579

6/5/4Cd
Richard
LINDOP
**Wybunbury**
*55M1525*

Cf
Margaret
PARROT
<1557-1575>
**Wybunbury**
*55M211*

=  1571

6/5/7Db
John
LINDOP
(1580>
*580258*

6/5/8Da
William
LINDOP
(1582-1650?
*582259*

6/5/9Da
Richard
LINDOP
(1583-1662)
*583260*

6/5/10Da
Thomas
LINDOP
(1584-1634)
*584113*

De
Cicile
LINDOP
(1585>
*585263*

Df
Jane
LINDOP
(1586>
*586264*

Dg
Margaret
LINDOP
(1587>
*587265*

Dh
Anne
LINDOP
(1588>
*588266*

**Wybunbury**

Ea
8 sons
2 daughters

Eb
1 son
3 daughters

Ec
4 sons
2 daughters

Ec
2 sons
2 daughters

# Pedigree 6/5/7

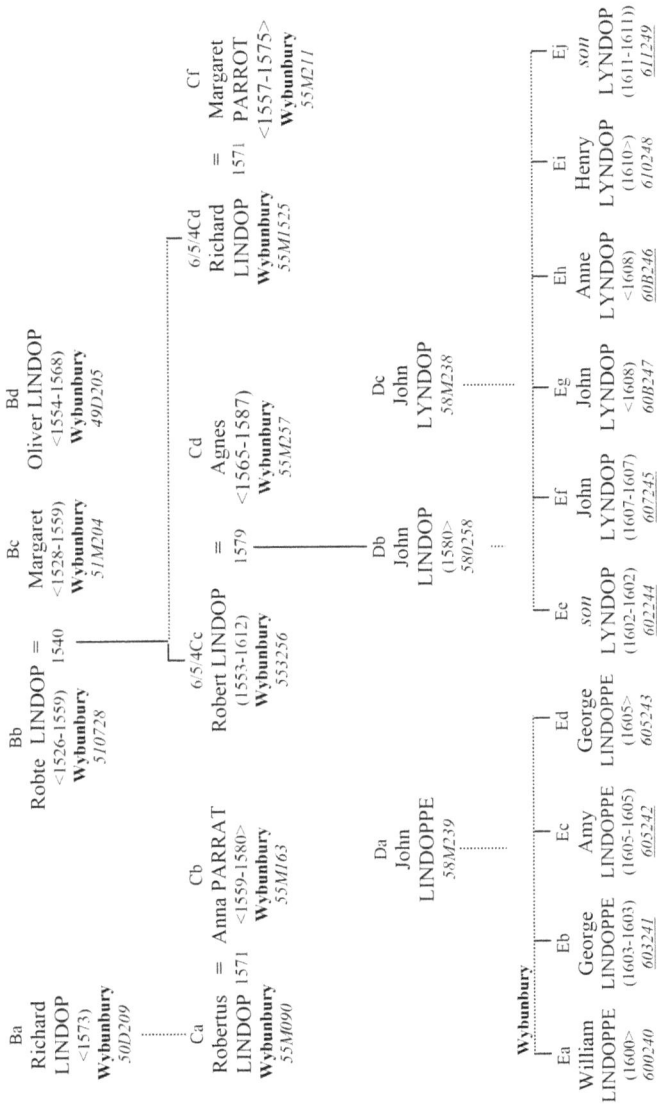

Ba
Richard
LINDOP
<1573)
**Wybunbury**
*50D209*

Bb
Robte LINDOP = 1540
<1526-1559)
**Wybunbury**
*510728*

Bc
Margaret
<1528-1559)
**Wybunbury**
*51M204*

Bd
Oliver LINDOP
<1554-1568)
**Wybunbury**
*49D205*

Cf
Margaret
PARROT
<1557-1575>
**Wybunbury**
*55M211*

Ca

Cb
Robertus = Anna PARRAT
LINDOP 1571    <1559-1580>
**Wybunbury**          **Wybunbury**
*55M090*              *55M163*

6:54Cc
Robert LINDOP
(1553-1612)
**Wybunbury**
*553256*

Cd
Agnes
<1565-1587)
**Wybunbury**
*55M257*

= 1579

6:54Cd
Richard
LINDOP
**Wybunbury**
*55M1525*

= 1571

Da
John
LINDOPPE
*58M239*

Db
John
LINDOP
(1580>
*580258*

Dc
John
LYNDOP
*58M238*

**Wybunbury**

Ea
William
LINDOPPE
(1600>
*600240*

Eb
George
LINDOPPE
(1603-1603)
*60324l*

Ec
Amy
LINDOPPE
(1605-1605)
*605242*

Ed
George
LINDOPPE
(1605>
*605243*

Ec
son
LYNDOP
(1602-1602)
*602244*

Ef
John
LYNDOP
(1607-1607)
*607245*

Eg
John
LYNDOP
<1608)
*60B247*

Eh
Anne
LYNDOP
<1608)
*60B246*

Ei
Henry
LYNDOP
(1610>
*610248*

Ej
son
LYNDOP
(1611-1611))
*611249*

# Pedigree 6/5/8

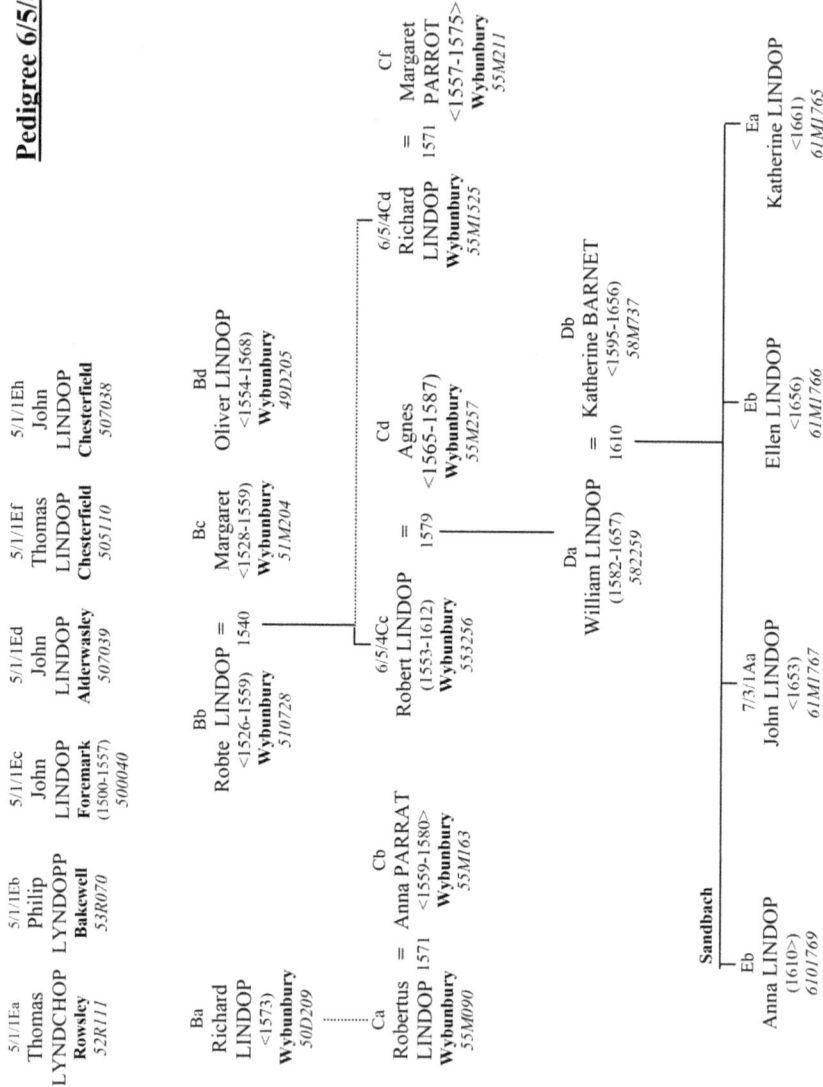

**5/1/1Ea**
Thomas
LYNDCHOP
**Rowsley**
*52R111*

**5/1/1Eb**
Philip
LYNDOPP
**Bakewell**
*53R070*

**5/1/1Ec**
John
LINDOP
**Foremark**
(1500-1557)
*500040*

**5/1/1Ed**
John
LINDOP
**Alderwasley**
*507039*

**5/1/1Ef**
Thomas
LINDOP
**Chesterfield**
*505110*

**5/1/1Eh**
John
LINDOP
**Chesterfield**
*507038*

**Ba**
Richard
LINDOP
<1573>
**Wybunbury**
*50D209*

**Bb**
Robte  LINDOP  =
<1526-1559)  1540
**Wybunbury**
*510728*

**Bc**
Margaret
<1528-1559)
**Wybunbury**
*51M204*

**Bd**
Oliver LINDOP
<1554-1568)
**Wybunbury**
*49D205*

**Ca**
Robertus  =  Anna PARRAT
LINDOP  1571  <1559-1580>
**Wybunbury**  **Wybunbury**
*55M090*  *55M163*

**Cb**

**6/5/4Cc**
Robert LINDOP
(1553-1612)
**Wybunbury**
*553256*

**Cd**
Agnes
<1565-1587)
**Wybunbury**
*55M257*

=
1579

**6/5/4Cd**
Richard
LINDOP
**Wybunbury**
*55M1525*

**Cf**
Margaret
PARROT
<1557-1575>
**Wybunbury**
*55M211*

=  1571

**Da**
William LINDOP
(1582-1657)
*582259*

**Db**
=  Katherine BARNET
1610  <1595-1656>
*58M737*

**Sandbach**

**Eb**
Anna LINDOP
(1610>)
*6101769*

**7/3/1Aa**
John LINDOP
<1653)
*61M1767*

**Eb**
Ellen LINDOP
<1656)
*61M1766*

**Ea**
Katherine LINDOP
<1661)
*61M1765*

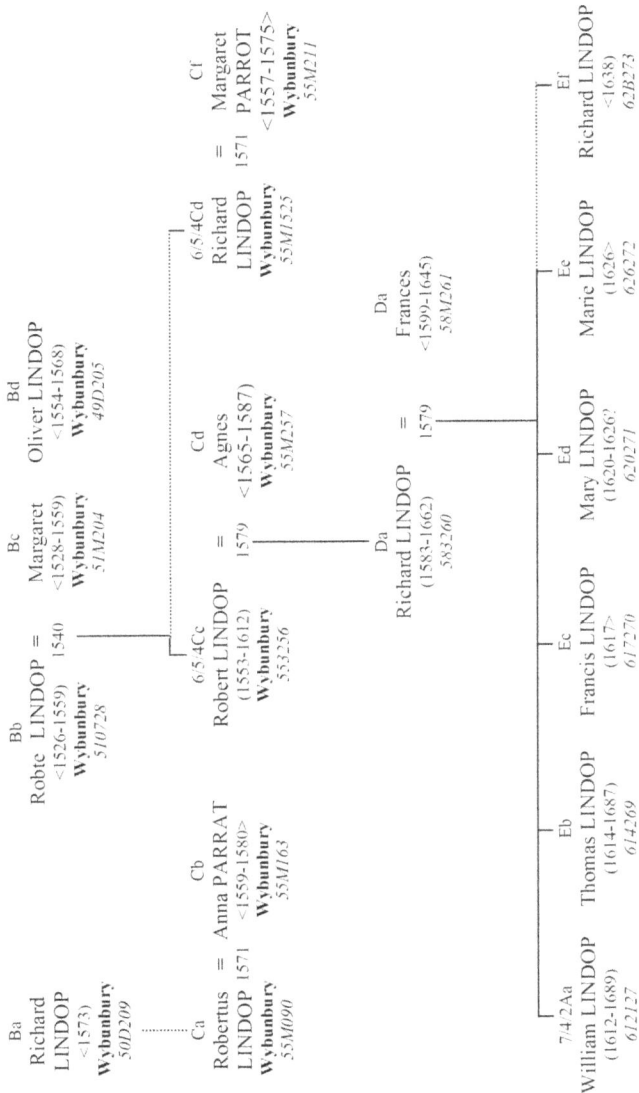

5/1/1Ea
Thomas
LYNDCHOP
**Rowsley**
*52R111*

5/1/1b
Philip
LYNDOPP
**Bakewell**
*53R070*

5/1/1Ec
John
LINDOP
**Foremark**
(1500-1557)
*500040*

5/1/1Ed
John
LINDOP
**Alderwasley**
*507039*

5/1/1Ef
Thomas
LINDOP
**Chesterfield**
*505110*

5/1/1Eh
John
LINDOP
**Chesterfield**
*507088*

Ba
Richard
LINDOP
<1573>
**Wybunbury**
*50D209*

Bb
Robte  LINDOP  =  1540
<1526-1559>
**Wybunbury**
*510728*

Bc
Margaret
<1528-1559>
**Wybunbury**
*51M204*

Bd
Oliver LINDOP
<1554-1568>
**Wybunbury**
*49D205*

Cf
Margaret
PARROT
<1557-1575>
**Wybunbury**
*55M211*

Ca
Robertus  =  Anna PARRAT
LINDOP  1571  <1559-1580>
**Wybunbury**    **Wybunbury**
*55M090*        *55M163*

Cb

6:5:4Cc
Robert LINDOP
(1553-1612)
**Wybunbury**
*553256*

Cd
Agnes
<1565-1587>
**Wybunbury**
*55M257*

=
1579

6:5:4Cd
Richard
LINDOP
**Wybunbury**
*55M1525*

=  1571

Da
Richard LINDOP
(1583-1662)
*583260*

=
1579

Da
Frances
<1599-1645>
*58M261*

7:4:2Aa
William LINDOP
(1612-1689)
*612127*

Eb
Thomas LINDOP
(1614-1687)
*614269*

Ec
Francis LINDOP
(1617>
*617270*

Ed
Mary LINDOP
(1620-1626?)
*620271*

Ee
Marie LINDOP
(1626>
*626272*

Ef
Richard LINDOP
<1638>
*62B273*

# Pedigree 6/5/10

5/1/1Ea
Thomas
LYNDCHOP
**Rowsley**
*52R111*

5/1/1Eb
Philip
LYNDOPP
**Bakewell**
*53R070*

5/1/1Ec
John
LINDOP
**Foremark**
(1500-1557)
*500040*

5/1/1Ed
John
LINDOP
**Alderwasley**
*507039*

5/1/1Ef
Thomas
LINDOP
**Chesterfield**
*505110*

5/1/1Eh
John
LINDOP
**Chesterfield**
*507038*

Ba
Richard
LINDOP
<1573>
**Wybunbury**
*50D209*

Bb
Robte  LINDOP  =  1540
<1526-1559)
**Wybunbury**
*510728*

Bc
Margaret
<1528-1559)
**Wybunbury**
*51M204*

Bd
Oliver LINDOP
<1554-1568)
**Wybunbury**
*49D205*

Ca
Robertus  =  Anna PARRAT
LINDOP  1571
**Wybunbury**
*55M090*

Cb
Anna PARRAT
<1559-1580>
**Wybunbury**
*55M163*

6/5/4Cc
Robert LINDOP  =
(1553-1612)
**Wybunbury**
*553256*

Cd
Agnes
<1565-1587)
**Wybunbury**
*55M257*

6/5/4Cd
Richard
LINDOP
**Wybunbury**
*55M525*

Cf
Margaret
PARROT
<1557-1575>
**Wybunbury**
*55M211*

=  1571

Da
Thomas LINDOP
(1584-1634)
*584113*

=  1579

b1     Db     b2
=  Margaret  =
*53M34*

Dc
Randal BATHOE
*53M335*

**Stretton, near Tilston**

**Chester**

Ea
Thomas LINDOP
(1621?-1634>
*621336*

Eb
Elizabeth LINDOP
(1623>
*623337*

7/5/6Bc
John LINDOP
(1626-1684>
*626044*

Ed
Sarah LINDOP
(1630>
*630105*

# Part 2

# 17th Century

Ab
Hester GLASSE
<1627-1625>
**Adbaston**
*61M462*

Ce
Ann SILVESTER

6/1/1Ei
Ferdinando LYNDOPPE
<1625-1646>
**Adbaston**
*61M461*

=
1639

=
1681

6/1/1Ec
William LYNDOP
(1596-1660)
**Eccleshall**
*5961289*

Cc
William LINDOPPE
(1639>
*639463*

Cd
Ferdinando
LINDOPPE
(1645 - 1748?)
*645465*

Dd
John LINDUP
(1693>

Cb
Katherine LINDOPPE
(1639>
*639463*

**Adbaston**

Ca
Margaret LINDOPPE
(1642-1661)
**Eccleshall**
*642174I*

Dc
Thomas LINDUP
(1686>
*6861650*

Dd
Sarah LINDUP
(1691>
*6911651*

Db
= Sarah SCLATER

**Broadwater**

Da
Ferdinando
LINDOPPE
<1695 - 1715>
*68M1649*

**Broadwater**

| Ea | Eb | Ec | Ed | Ef | Eg | Eh | Ei | Ej | Ek | El |
|---|---|---|---|---|---|---|---|---|---|---|
| Thomas | John | Sarah | Charles | Richard | Henry | Ferdinando | Charles | James John | Edward | Mary |
| (1710-1729) | (1711-1770) | (1713-1737) | (1716-1716) | (1717-1763) | (1718> | (1710-1729) | (1722> | (1723-1763) | (1727-1731) | (1729> |
| *7101653* | | *7101654* | | | | | | | | |

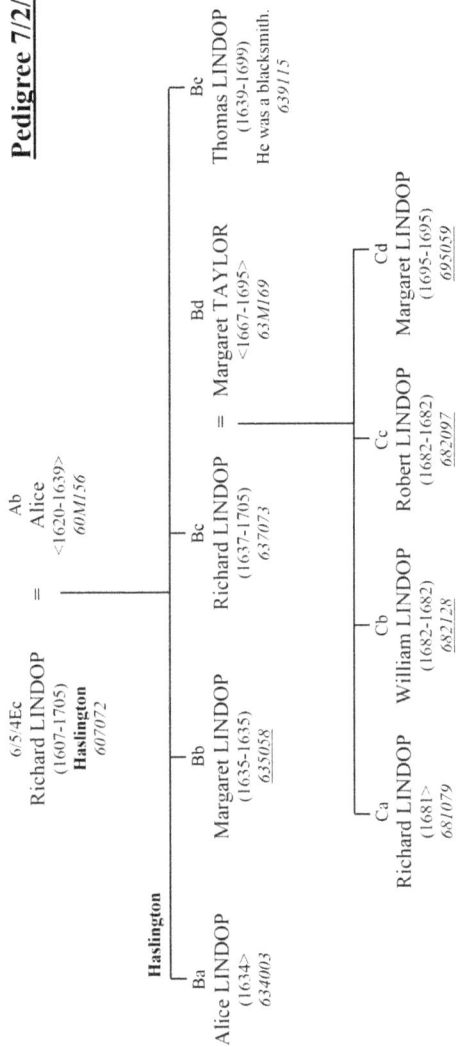

**Haslington**

Ba
Alice LINDOP
(1634>
634003

654Ec
Richard LINDOP
(1607-1705)
**Haslington**
607072

=

Ab
Alice
<1620-1639>
60M156

Bb
Margaret LINDOP
(1635-1635)
635058

Bc
Richard LINDOP
(1637-1705)
637073

=

Bd
Margaret TAYLOR
<1667-1695>
63M169

Bc
Thomas LINDOP
(1639-1699)
He was a blacksmith.
639115

Ca
Richard LINDOP
(1681>
681079

Cb
William LINDOP
(1682-1682)
682128

Cc
Robert LINDOP
(1682-1682)
682097

Cd
Margaret LINDOP
(1695-1695)
695059

**Pedigree 7/3/1**

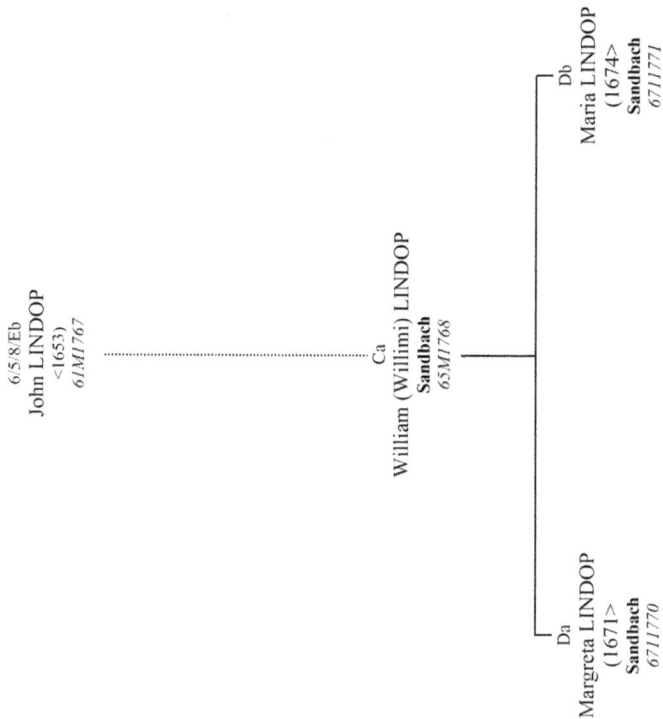

6/5/8/Eb
John LINDOP
<1653)
*61M1767*

Ca
William (Willimi) LINDOP
**Sandbach**
*65M1768*

Db
Maria LINDOP
(1674>
**Sandbach**
*6711771*

Da
Margreta LINDOP
(1671>
**Sandbach**
*6711770*

# Pedigree 7/4/1

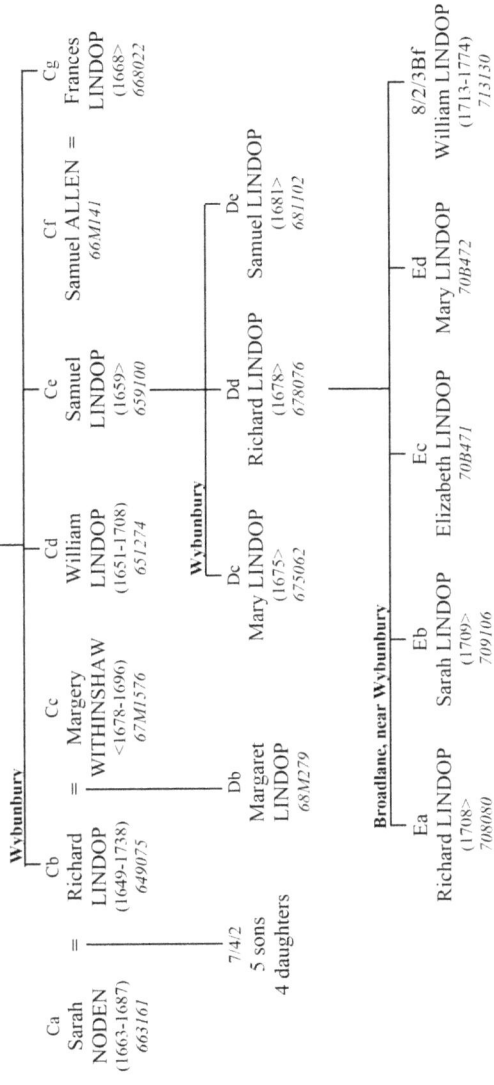

Margery could be
William's second wife.

**6.5/9Ea**
William LINDOP
(1612-1689)
*612127*

**Ab**
Margery LATHAM
<1637-1678>
*61M268*

= 1679

**Ca**
Sarah
NODEN
(1663-1687)
*663161*

=

**7/4/2**
5 sons
4 daughters

**Wybunbury**

**Cb**
Richard
LINDOP
(1649-1738)
*649075*

=

**Cc**
Margery
WITHINSHAW
<1678-1696>
*67M1576*

**Db**
Margaret
LINDOP
*68M279*

**Cd**
William
LINDOP
(1651-1708)
*651274*

**Ce**
Samuel
LINDOP
(1659>
*659100*

**Cf**
Samuel ALLEN =

*66M141*

**Cg**
Frances
LINDOP
(1668>
*668022*

**Wybunbury**

**Dc**
Mary LINDOP
(1675>
*675062*

**Dd**
Richard LINDOP
(1678>
*678076*

**De**
Samuel LINDOP
(1681>
*681102*

**Broadlane, near Wybunbury**

**Ea**
Richard LINDOP
(1708>
*708080*

**Eb**
Sarah LINDOP
(1709>
*709106*

**Ec**
Elizabeth LINDOP
*70B471*

**Ed**
Mary LINDOP
*70B472*

**8/2/3Bf**
William LINDOP
(1713-1774)
*713130*

# Pedigree 7/4/2

Margery could be William's second wife.

6/5/9Ea
William LINDOP (1612-1689) *612127*
= 1679 = Margery LATHAM <1637-1678> *61M268*

[P]

| | | | |
|---|---|---|---|
| a | b | c | d |
| Richard LINDOP (1649-1738) *649075* | William LINDOP (1651-1708) *651274* | Samuel LINDOP (1659> ↓ *7/4/1* | Frances LINDOP (1668> *668022* [P] |

Samuel ALLEN = Frances LINDOP *66MI41*

**Wybunbury**

Richard LINDOP = Sarah NODEN (1663-1687) *663161*

[Q]

| | | | | | | | | |
|---|---|---|---|---|---|---|---|---|
| a | b | c | d | e | f | g | h | i |
| Robert LINDOP (1675-1720) *675276* | Richard LINDOP (1676-1726?) *676078* | Sarah LINDOP (1677> *677278* | Ellen LINDOP (1679> *679017* | Thomas LINDOP (1681> *681117* | Margery LINDOP (1682> *682061* | Peter LINDOP (1685-1705) *685069* | Samuel LINDOP (1687> *687101* | Hannah LINDOP (1688> *688025* [Q] |

**Wybunbury**

Richard LINDOP

[R]

| | | | |
|---|---|---|---|
| a | b | c | d |
| Sarah LINDOP (1709> *709106* [R] | Richard LINDOP (1710-1781) *710281* | William LINDOP (1713-1774) *713282* ↓ | Samuel LINDOP (1715-1715) *715284* [R] |

# Pedigree 7/5/1

**Chester**

6/5/10Da
Thomas LINDOP
(1584-1634)
*584113*

b1 =

6/5/10Db
Margaret
*53M334*

b2 =

6/5/10Dc
Randal BATHOE
*53M335*

**Stretton, near Tilston**

6/5/10Ea
Thomas LINDOP
(1621?-1634>)
*621336*

=

6/5/10Eb
Elizabeth LINDOP
(1623>)
*633337*

6/5/10Ec
John LINDOP
(1626-1684>)
*626044*

=

Bd
Elizabeth
<1640-1684>
*63M338*

6/5/10Ed
Sarah LINDOP
(1630>)
*630105*

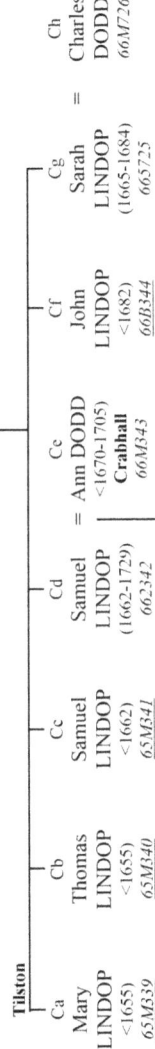
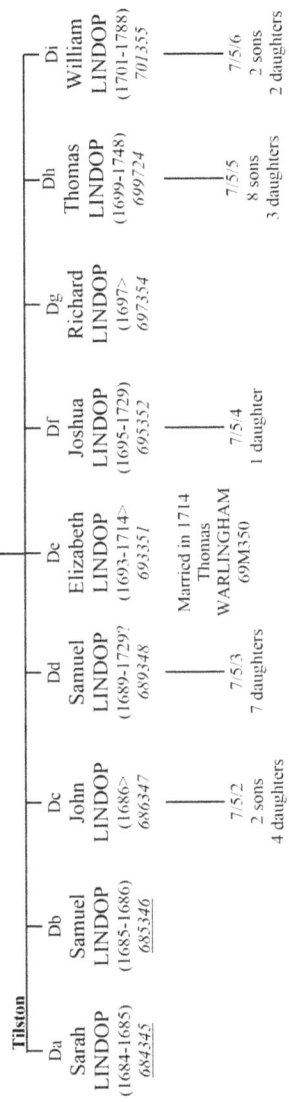

**Tilston**

Ca
Mary LINDOP
<1655)
*65M339*

Cb
Thomas LINDOP
<1655)
*65M340*

Cc
Samuel LINDOP
<1662)
*65M341*

Cd
Samuel LINDOP
(1662-1729)
*662342*

=

Ce
Ann DODD
<1670-1705>
**Crabhall**
*66M343*

Cf
John LINDOP
<1682)
*66B344*

Cg
Sarah LINDOP
(1665-1684)
*665725*

=

Ch
Charles DODD
(1630>)
*66M726*

**Tilston**

Da
Sarah LINDOP
(1684-1685)
*684345*

Db
Samuel LINDOP
(1685-1686)
*685346*

Dc
John LINDOP
(1686>)
*686347*

7/5/2
2 sons
4 daughters

Dd
Samuel LINDOP
(1689-1729?)
*689348*

7/5/3
7 daughters

De
Elizabeth LINDOP
(1693-1714>)
*693351*

Married in 1714
Thomas
WARLINGHAM
*69M350*

Df
Joshua LINDOP
(1695-1729)
*695352*

7/5/4
1 daughter

Dg
Richard LINDOP
(1697>)
*697354*

Dh
Thomas LINDOP
(1699-1748)
*699724*

7/5/5
8 sons
3 daughters

Di
William LINDOP
(1701-1788)
*701355*

7/5/6
2 sons
2 daughters

| | 6/5/10Da | | b1 | 6/5/10Db | b2 | | 6/5/10Dc | | | | 6/5/10Ed |
|---|---|---|---|---|---|---|---|---|---|---|---|
| | Thomas LINDOP | | = | Margaret | = | | Randal BATHOE | | | | Sarah LINDOP |
| | (1584-1634) | | | *53M334* | | | *53M335* | | | | (1630> |
| | *584113* | | | | | | | | | | *630105* |

**Stretton, near Tilston**

| 6/5/10Ea | 6/5/10Eb | | | | | 6/5/10Ec | Bd | | Cg | | Ch |
|---|---|---|---|---|---|---|---|---|---|---|---|
| Thomas LINDOP | Elizabeth LINDOP | | | | | John LINDOP | Elizabeth | | Sarah | = | Charles |
| (1621?-1634> | (1623> | | | | | (1626-1684> | <1640-1684> | | LINDOP | | DODD |
| *621336* | *623337* | | | | | *626044* | *63M338* | | (1665-1684) | | *66M726* |
| | | | | | | | | | *665725* | | |

**Tilston**

| Ca | Cb | Cc | Cd | Ce | | Cf | | 7/5/1Dg | 7/5/5Dh | | 7/5/6Di |
|---|---|---|---|---|---|---|---|---|---|---|---|
| Mary | Thomas | Samuel | Samuel | Ann DODD | = | John | | Richard | Thomas | | William |
| LINDOP | LINDOP | LINDOP | LINDOP | <1670-1705) | | LINDOP | | LINDOP | LINDOP | | LINDOP |
| <1655> | <1655) | <1662) | (1662-1729) | **Crabhall** | | <1682) | | (1718> | (1699-1748) | | (1701-1788) |
| *65M339* | *65M340* | *65M341* | *662342* | *66M343* | | *66B344* | | *718633* | *699724* | | *701355* |

**Tilston**

| 7/5/1Da | 7/5/1Db | | Dc | | Dd | 7/5/3Dd | 7/5/1De | | 7/5/4Df | | |
|---|---|---|---|---|---|---|---|---|---|---|---|
| Sarah | Samuel | | John | = | Frances | Samuel | Elizabeth | | Joshua | | |
| | | | LINDOP | 1710 | *68M635* | LINDOP | LINDOP | | LINDOP | | |
| | | | (1686> | | | (1689-1729? | (1693-1714> | | (1695-1729) | | |
| | | | *686347* | | | *689348* | *693351* | | *695352* | | |

**Edge, near Malpas**

| Ea | Eb | | Ec | Ed | | Ee | | Ef |
|---|---|---|---|---|---|---|---|---|
| Anna LINDOP | John LINDOP | | Elizabeth LINDOP | Samuel LINDOP | | Mary LINDOP | | Anna LINDOP |
| (1711> | (1713-1723) | | (1714-1731) | (1716> | | (1718> | | (1720-1730> |
| *711629* | *713630* | | *714631* | *716632* | | *718633* | | *720634* |

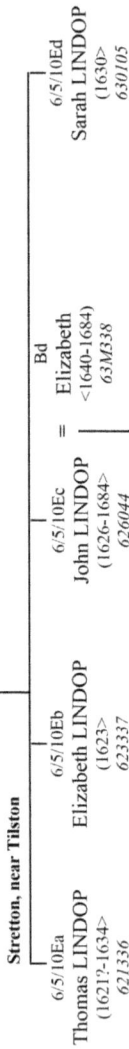
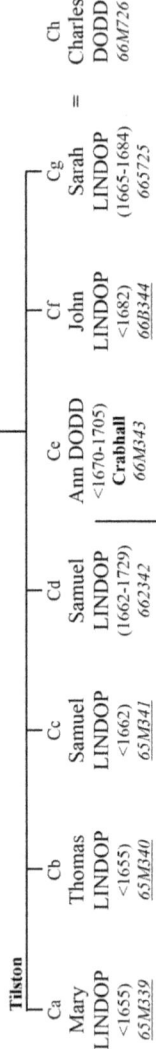
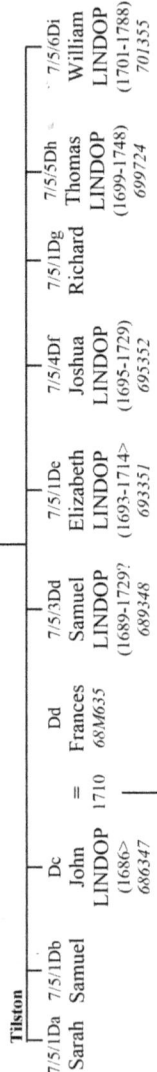
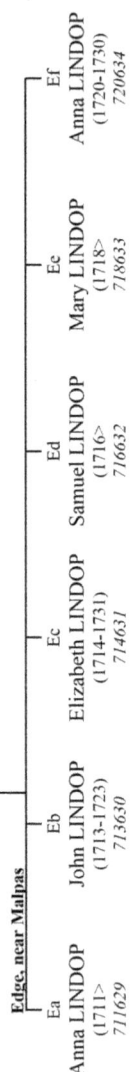

# Pedigree 7/5/3

6/5/10Da
Thomas LINDOP
(1584-1634)
*584113*

b1 = 6/5/10Db Margaret *53M334*

b2 = 6/5/10Dc Randal BATHOE *53M335*

**Stretton, near Tilston**

6/5/10Ea
Thomas LINDOP
(1621?-1634>)
*621336*

6/5/10Eb
Elizabeth LINDOP
(1623>)
*623337*

6/5/10Ec
John LINDOP
(1626-1684>)
*626044*
=
Bd
Elizabeth
<1640-1684>
*63M338*

6/5/10Ed
Sarah LINDOP
(1630>)
*630105*
=
Ch
Charles
DODD
*66M726*

**Tilston**

Ca
Mary
LINDOP
<1655>
*65M339*

Cb
Thomas
LINDOP
<1655>
*65M340*

Cc
Samuel
LINDOP
<1662>
*65M341*

Cd
Samuel
LINDOP
(1662-1729)
*662342*

Ce
Ann DODD
<1670-1705>
**Crabhall**
*66M343*
=

Cf
John
LINDOP
<1682>
*66B344*

Cg
Sarah
LINDOP
(1665-1684)
*665725*

**Tilston**

7/5/1Da Sarah   7/5/1Db Samuel

7/5/2Dc
John
LINDOP
(1686>)
*686347*

7/5/3Dd
Samuel
LINDOP
(1689-1729?)
*689348*
= 1713

De
Mary
CLUBS
*68M349*

Ec
Anne
LINDOP
(1718)
*718649*

Ed
Anne
LINDOP
(1720>)
*720650*

7/5/1De
Elizabeth
LINDOP
(1693-1714>)
*693351*

Ee
Martha
LINDOP
(1720>)
*720671*
Married Thomas
CAPPUR in 1742

7/5/4Df
Joshua
LINDOP
(1695-1729)
*695352*

7/5/1Dg
Richard
LINDOP

7/5/5Dh
Thomas
LINDOP
(1699-1748)
*699724*

7/5/6Di
William
LINDOP
(1701-1788)
*701355*

**Shocklach, near Tilston**

Ea
Frances
LINDOP
(1714>)
*714647*

Eb
Mary
LINDOP
(1716-1740)
*716648*
Married Thomas
HOUGLAND in 1740

Ef
Sarah
LINDOP
(1722>)
*722676*

Eg
Elizabeth
LINDOP
(1722-1741)
*722675*

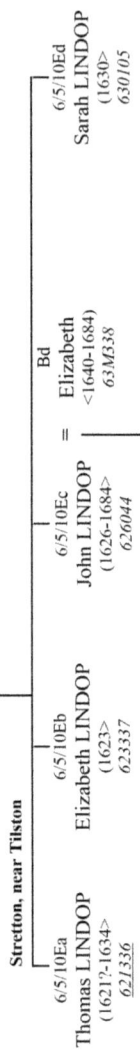
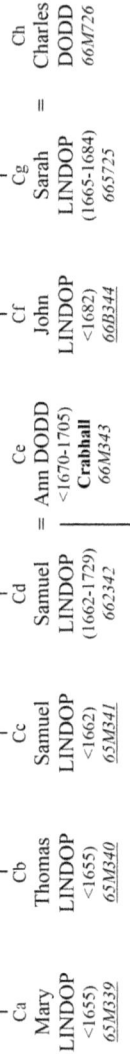
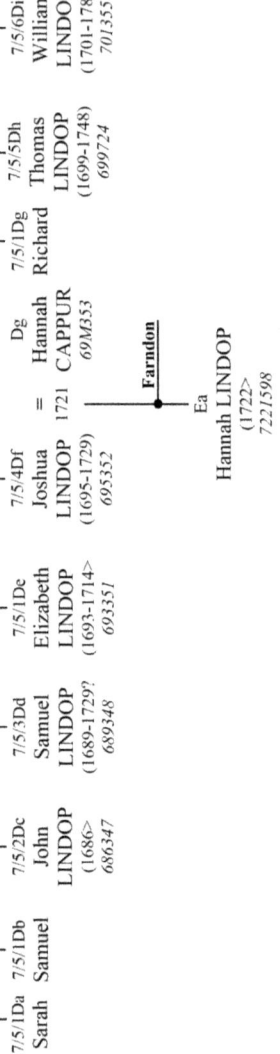

6/5/10Da
Thomas LINDOP
(1584-1634)
*584113*

b1   6/5/10Db
=   Margaret

*53M334*

b2
=

6/5/10Dc
Randal BATHOE
*53M335*

**Stretton, near Tilston**

6/5/10Ea
Thomas LINDOP
(1621?-1634>)
*621336*

6/5/10Eb
Elizabeth LINDOP
(1623)
*623337*

Bd
Elizabeth
<1640-1684>
*63M338*

=

6/5/10Ec
John LINDOP
(1626-1684>)
*620044*

6/5/10Ed
Sarah LINDOP
(1630>)
*630105*

**Tilston**

Ca
Mary
LINDOP
<1655)
*65M339*

Cb
Thomas
LINDOP
<1655)
*65M340*

Cc
Samuel
LINDOP
<1662)
*65M341*

Cd
Samuel
LINDOP
(1662-1729)
*662342*

Ce
Ann DODD
<1670-1705)
**Crabhall**
*66M343*

=

Cf
John
LINDOP
<1682)
*66B344*

Cg
Sarah
LINDOP
(1665-1684)
*665725*

Ch
Charles
DODD
*66M726*

=

**Tilston**

7/5/1Da
Sarah

7/5/1Db
Samuel

7/5/2Dc
John
LINDOP
(1686<)
*686347*

7/5/3Dd
Samuel
LINDOP
(1689-1729?)
*689348*

7/5/1De
Elizabeth
LINDOP
(1693-1714>)
*693351*

7/5/4Df
Joshua
LINDOP
(1695-1729)
*695352*

=   1721

Dg
Hannah
CAPPUR
*69M353*

7/5/1Dg
Richard

7/5/5Dh
Thomas
LINDOP
(1699-1748)
*699724*

7/5/6Di
William
LINDOP
(1701-1788)
*701355*

**Farndon**

Ea
Hannah LINDOP
(1722>)
*7221598*

# Pedigree 7/5/5

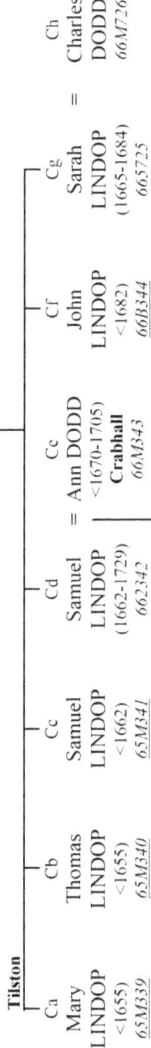
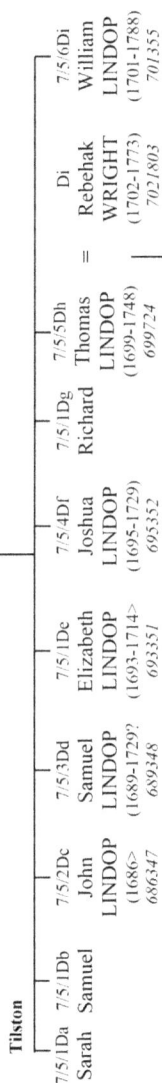
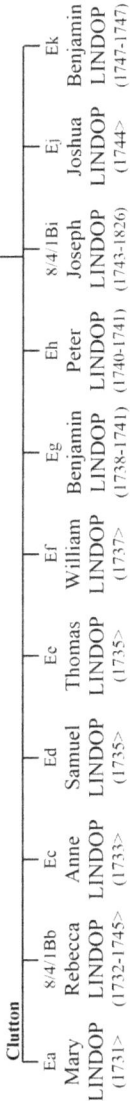

6/5/10Da Thomas LINDOP (1584-1634) *584/13*

b1 = 6/5/10Db Margaret *53M334*

b2 = 6/5/10Dc Randal BATHOE *53M335*

**Stretton, near Tilston**

6/5/10Ea Thomas LINDOP (1621?-1634>) *621336*

6/5/10Eb Elizabeth LINDOP (1623>) *623337*

6/5/10Ec John LINDOP (1626-1684>) *626044*
= Bd Elizabeth <1640-1684> *63M338*

6/5/10Ed Sarah LINDOP (1630>) *630105*
= Ch Charles DODD *66M726*

**Tilston**

Ca Mary LINDOP <1655> *65M339*

Cb Thomas LINDOP <1655> *65M340*

Cc Samuel LINDOP <1662> *65M341*

Cd Samuel LINDOP (1662-1729) *662342*
= Cc Ann DODD <1670-1705) **Crabhall** *66M343*

Cf John LINDOP <1682> *66B344*

Cg Sarah LINDOP (1665-1684) *665725*

**Tilston**

7/5/1Da Sarah

7/5/1Db Samuel

7/5/2Dc John LINDOP (1686>) *686347*

7/5/3Dd Samuel LINDOP (1689-1729?) *689348*

7/5/1De Elizabeth LINDOP (1693-1714>) *693351*

7/5/4Df Joshua LINDOP (1695-1729) *695352*

7/5/1Dg Richard

7/5/5Dh Thomas LINDOP (1699-1748) *699724*
= Di Rebehak WRIGHT (1702-1773) *702/803*

7/5/6Di William LINDOP (1701-1788) *701355*

**Clutton**

Ea Mary LINDOP (1731>)

8/4/1Bb Rebecca LINDOP (1732-1745>)

Ec Anne LINDOP (1733>)

Ed Samuel LINDOP (1735>)

Ec Thomas LINDOP (1735>)

Ef William LINDOP (1737>)

Eg Benjamin LINDOP (1738-1741)

Eh Peter LINDOP (1740-1741)

8/4/1Bi Joseph LINDOP (1743-1826)

Ej Joshua LINDOP (1744>)

Ek Benjamin LINDOP (1747-1747)

# Pedigree 7/5/6

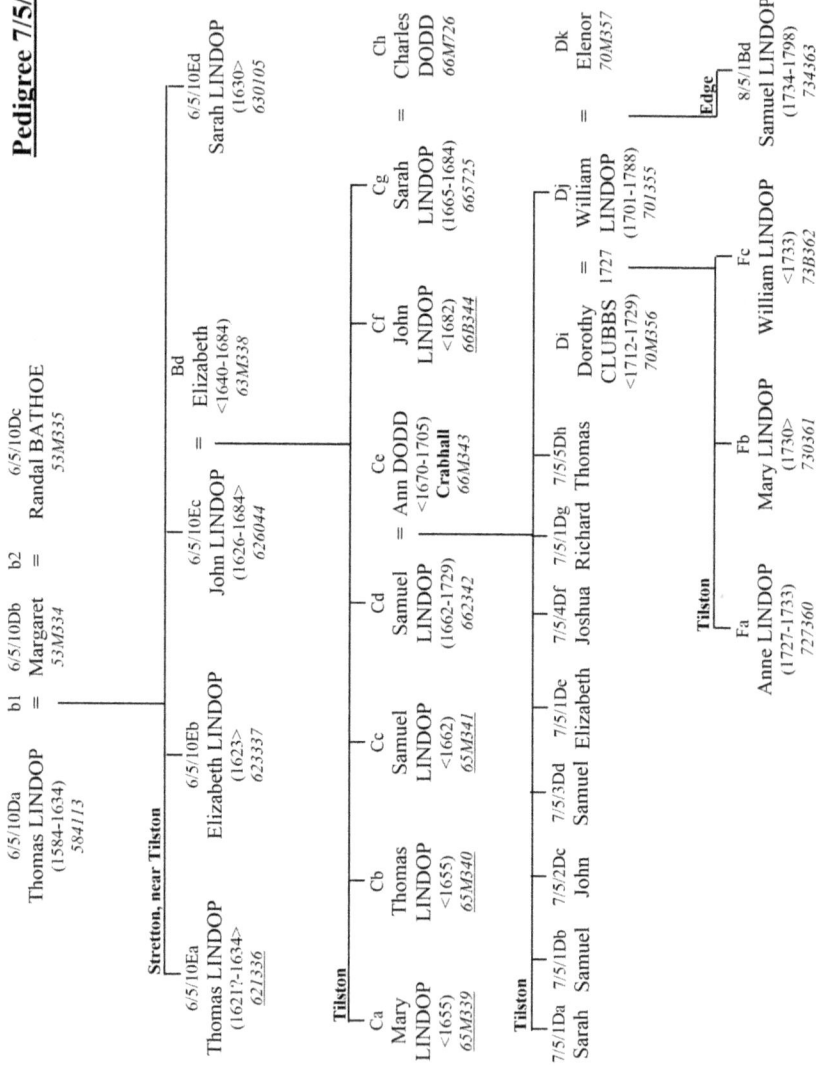

6/5/10Da
**Thomas LINDOP**
(1584-1634)
*584I13*

b1  6/5/10Db
= **Margaret**
*53M334*

b2  6/5/10Dc
= **Randal BATHOE**
*53M335*

**Stretton, near Tilston**

6/5/10Ea
**Thomas LINDOP**
(1621?-1634>)
*621336*

6/5/10Eb
**Elizabeth LINDOP**
(1623>)
*623337*

6/5/10Ec
**John LINDOP**
(1626-1684>)
*626044*

Bd
= **Elizabeth**
<1640-1684>
*63M338*

6/5/10Ed
**Sarah LINDOP**
(1630>)
*630I05*

Ch
= **Charles DODD**
*66M726*

**Tilston**

Ca
**Mary LINDOP**
<1655>
*65M339*

Cb
**Thomas LINDOP**
<1655>
*65M340*

Cc
**Samuel LINDOP**
<1662>
*65M341*

Cd
**Samuel LINDOP**
(1662-1729)
*662342*

Ce
= **Ann DODD**
<1670-1705>
Crabhall
*66M343*

Cf
**John LINDOP**
<1682>
*66B344*

Cg
**Sarah LINDOP**
(1665-1684)
*665725*

**Tilston**

7/5/1Da  Sarah
7/5/1Db  Samuel
7/5/2Dc  John
7/5/3Dd  Samuel
7/5/1De  Elizabeth
7/5/4Df  Joshua
7/5/1Dg  Richard
7/5/5Dh  Thomas

Di
**Dorothy CLUBBS**
<1712-1729>
*70M356*

= 1727

Dj
**William LINDOP**
(1701-1788)
*70I355*

Dk
= **Elenor**
*70M357*

**Tilston**

Fa
**Anne LINDOP**
(1727-1733)
*727360*

Fb
**Mary LINDOP**
(1730>)
*730361*

Fc
**William LINDOP**
<1733>
*73B362*

**Edge**

8/5/1Bd
**Samuel LINDOP**
(1734-1798)
*734363*

# Part 3

# 18<sup>th</sup> Century

# Pedigree 8/1/1

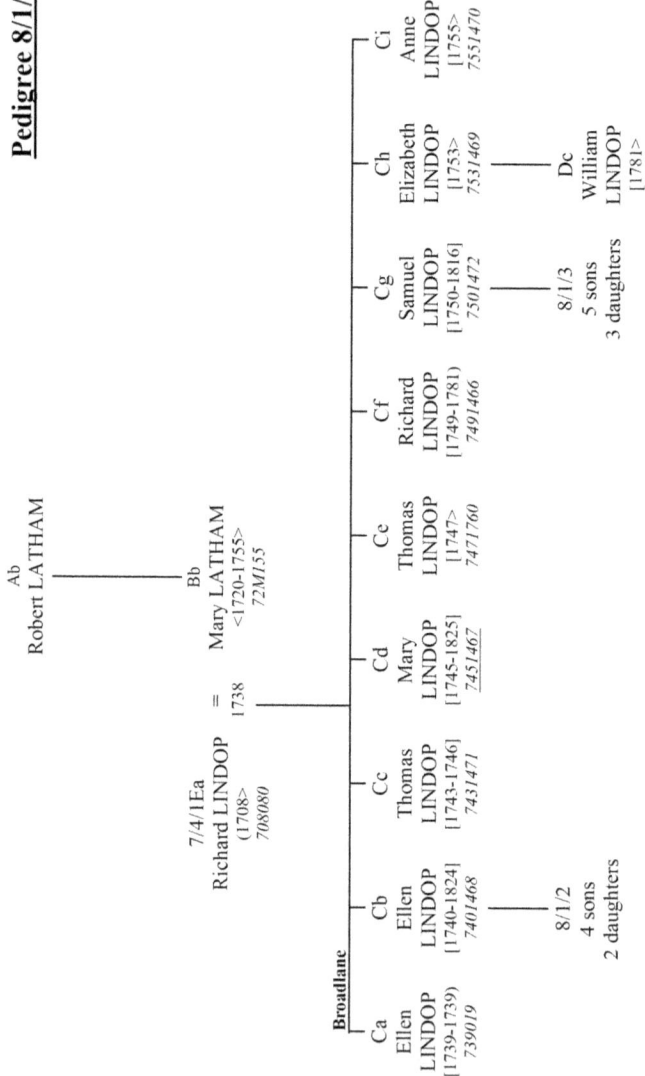

Ab
Robert LATHAM

Bb
Mary LATHAM
<1720-1755>
72M155

7/4/1Ea        =
Richard LINDOP    1738
(1708>
708080

**Broadlane**

Ca
Ellen
LINDOP
[1739-1739)
739019

Cb
Ellen
LINDOP
[1740-1824)
740/468

8/1/2
4 sons
2 daughters

Cc
Thomas
LINDOP
[1743-1746)
743/471

Cd
Mary
LINDOP
[1745-1825]
745/467

Ce
Thomas
LINDOP
[1747>
747/760

Cf
Richard
LINDOP
[1749-1781)
749/466

Cg
Samuel
LINDOP
[1750-1816]
750/472

8/1/3
5 sons
3 daughters

Ch
Elizabeth
LINDOP
[1753>
753/469

Dc
William
LINDOP
[1781>

Ci
Anne
LINDOP
[1755>
755/470

Ab
Robert LATHAM

Bb
Mary LATHAM
<1720-1755>
72M/55

7/4/1Ea
Richard LINDOP
(1708>
708080

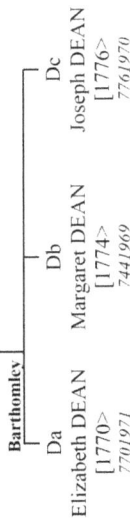

=
1738

| 8/1/1Ca | 8/1/1Cc | 8/1/1Cd | 8/1/1Ce | 8/1/1Cf | 8/1/1Cg | 8/1/1Ch | 8/1/1Ci |
|---------|---------|---------|---------|---------|---------|-----------|------|
| Ellen | Thomas | Mary | Thomas | Richard | Samuel | Elizabeth | Anne |

**Broadlane**

Cb
Ellen LINDOP
[1740-1824]
740/468

Ca
Joseph DEAN

=

**Barthomley**

| Da | Db | Dc |
|----|----|----|
| Elizabeth DEAN | Margaret DEAN | Joseph DEAN |
| [1770> | [1774> | [1776> |
| 770/971 | 744/969 | 776/970 |

# Pedigree 8/1/3

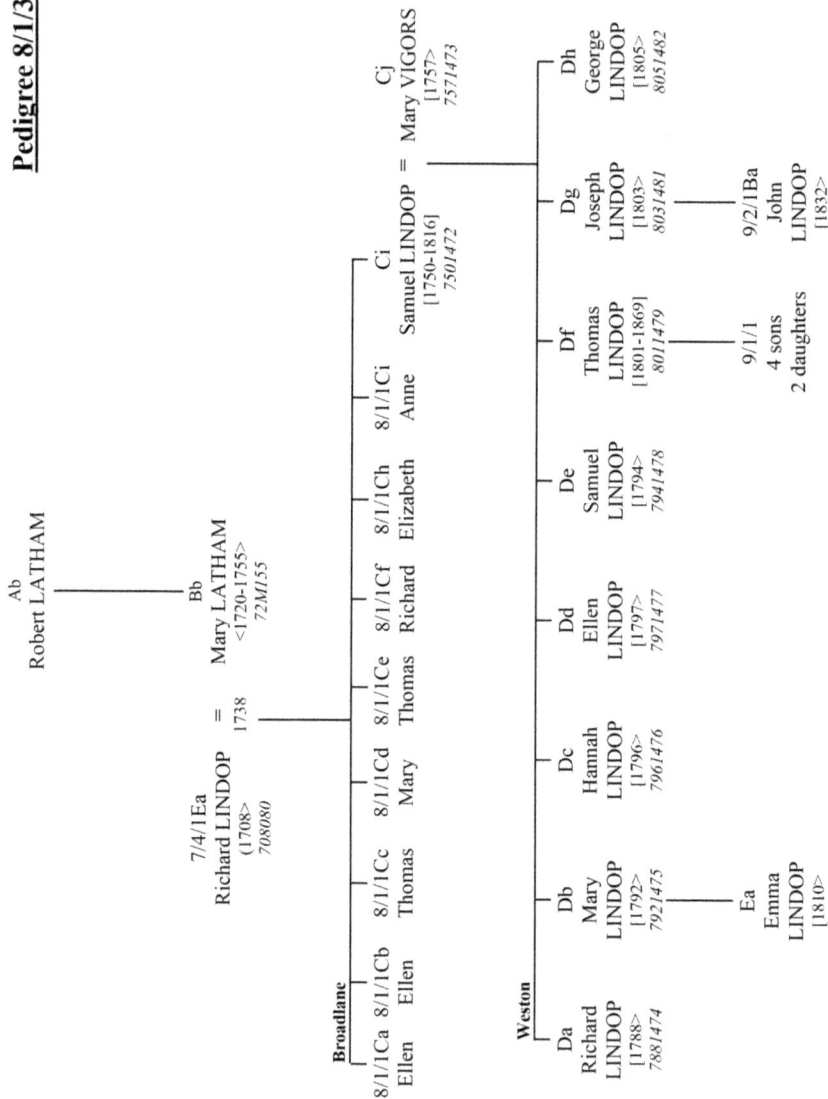

Ab
Robert LATHAM

Bb
Mary LATHAM
<1720-1755>
72MI55

7/4/1Ea
Richard LINDOP    =    1738
(1708>
708080

**Broadlane**

8/1/1Ca  8/1/1Cb    8/1/1Cc    8/1/1Cd    8/1/1Ce    8/1/1Cf    8/1/1Ch    8/1/1Ci
Ellen    Ellen      Thomas     Mary       Thomas     Richard    Elizabeth  Anne

Cj
Mary VIGORS
[1757>
7571473

Ci
Samuel LINDOP    =
[1750-1816]
7501472

**Weston**

Da
Richard
LINDOP
[1788>
7881474

Db
Mary
LINDOP
[1792>
7921475

Dc
Hannah
LINDOP
[1796>
7961476

Dd
Ellen
LINDOP
[1797>
7971477

De
Samuel
LINDOP
[1794>
7941478

Df
Thomas
LINDOP
[1801-1869]
8011479

Dg
Joseph
LINDOP
[1803>
8031481

Dh
George
LINDOP
[1805>
8051482

Ea
Emma
LINDOP
[1810>

9/1/1
4 sons
2 daughters

9/2/1Ba
John
LINDOP
[1832>

# Pedigree 8/2/1

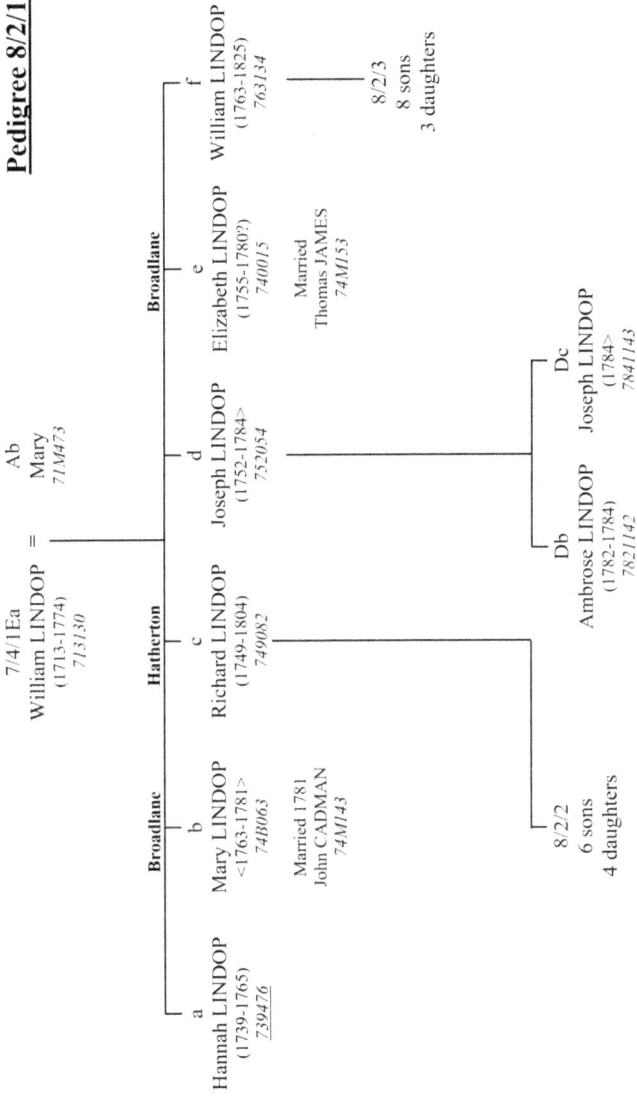

**Broadlane**

7/4/1Ea
William LINDOP
(1713-1774)
*713130*

Ab
Mary
*71M473*

**Broadlane**
a
Hannah LINDOP
(1739-1765)
*739476*

b
Mary LINDOP
<1763-1781>
*748063*

Married 1781
John CADMAN
*74M143*

**Hatherton**
c
Richard LINDOP
(1749-1804)
*749082*

d
Joseph LINDOP
(1752-1784>
*752054*

**Broadlane**
e
Elizabeth LINDOP
(1755-1780?)
*740015*

Married
Thomas JAMES
*74M153*

f
William LINDOP
(1763-1825)
*763134*

8/2/2
6 sons
4 daughters

Db
Ambrose LINDOP
(1782-1784)
*7821142*

Dc
Joseph LINDOP
(1784>
*7841143*

8/2/3
8 sons
3 daughters

# Pedigree 8/2/2

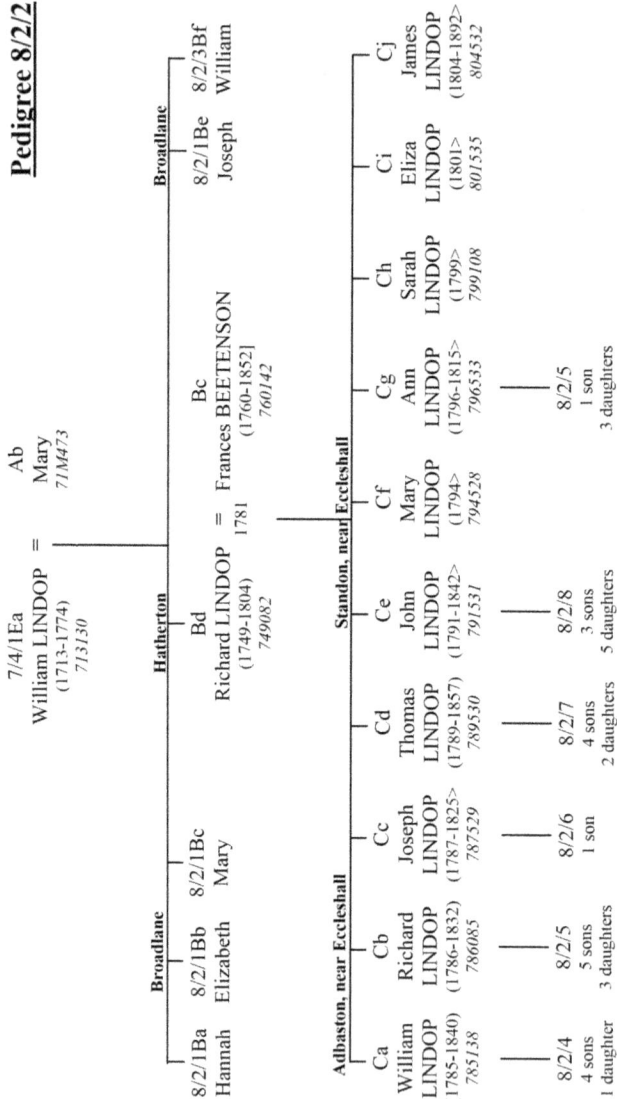

**Broadlane**

7/4/1Ea
William LINDOP = Ab
Mary
(1713-1774)  *71M473*
*713130*

**Broadlane**

8/2/1Ba       8/2/1Bb      8/2/1Bc
Hannah       Elizabeth    Mary

**Hatherton**

Bd
Richard LINDOP = Bc
(1749-1804)   1781   Frances BEETENSON
*749082*              (1760-1852]
                      *760142*

8/2/1Be    8/2/3Bf
Joseph     William

**Adbaston, near Eccleshall**

Ca
William
LINDOP
(1785-1840)
*785138*

Cb
Richard
LINDOP
(1786-1832)
*786085*

Cc
Joseph
LINDOP
(1787-1825>
*787529*

Cd
Thomas
LINDOP
(1789-1857)
*789530*

**Standon, near Eccleshall**

Ce
John
LINDOP
(1791-1842>
*791531*

Cf
Mary
LINDOP
(1794>
*794528*

Cg
Ann
LINDOP
(1796-1815>
*796533*

Ch
Sarah
LINDOP
(1799>
*799108*

Ci
Eliza
LINDOP
(1801>
*801535*

Cj
James
LINDOP
(1804-1892>
*804532*

8/2/4
4 sons
1 daughter

8/2/5
5 sons
3 daughters

8/2/6
1 son

8/2/7
4 sons
2 daughters

8/2/8
3 sons
5 daughters

8/2/5
1 son
3 daughters

# Pedigree 8/2/3

7/4/1Ea
William LINDOP
(1713-1774)
*713130*

Ab
Mary
*71M473*

=

**Broadlane**

Bf
William LINDOP
(1745-1825)
*745134*

=

Bg
Elizabeth LOCK
(1763-1838)
*763475*

**Broadlane**

8/2/1Ba
Hannah

Db
8/2/1Bb
Elizabeth

Dc
8/2/1Bc
Mary

**Hatherton**

8/2/2Bd
Richard

8/2/1Be
Joseph

8/2/2
6 sons
4 daughters

8/2/1
2 sons

**Adbaston, near Eccleshall**

**High Offley**

**Adbaston**

Da
Elizabeth
LINDOP
(1783>
*783016*

Married
Charles
GILBERT
*78M149*

Db
William
LINDOP
(1785-
1848)
*785139*

8/2/9
5 sons
2 daughters

Dc
Richard
LINDOP
(1785|
1785|
*785084*

Dd
Joseph
LINDOP
(1787-
1831>
*787056*

8/2/10
3 sons
4 daughters

De
Samuel
LINDOP
(1789-
1838)
*789103*

Married
Alice
BARKER
in 1827

Df
John
LINDOP
(1792-1851>
*792053*

8/2/11Dc
1 son
1 adopted
daughter

Dg
Ann
LINDOP
(1795-
1822>
*795007*

8/2/12
1 son
1 daughter

Dh
Mary
LINDOP
(1797-1823>
*797067*

Married
Abraham
HOPWOOD
In 1823
*80M151*

Di
Richard
LINDOP
(1801-
1813|
*801086*

Dj
Isaiah
LINDOP
(1805-
1872|
*805030*

8/2/11Dd
2 sons
1 daughter

Dk
George
LINDOP
(1801-
1846>
*801023*

8/2/13
4 sons

# Pedigree 8/2/4

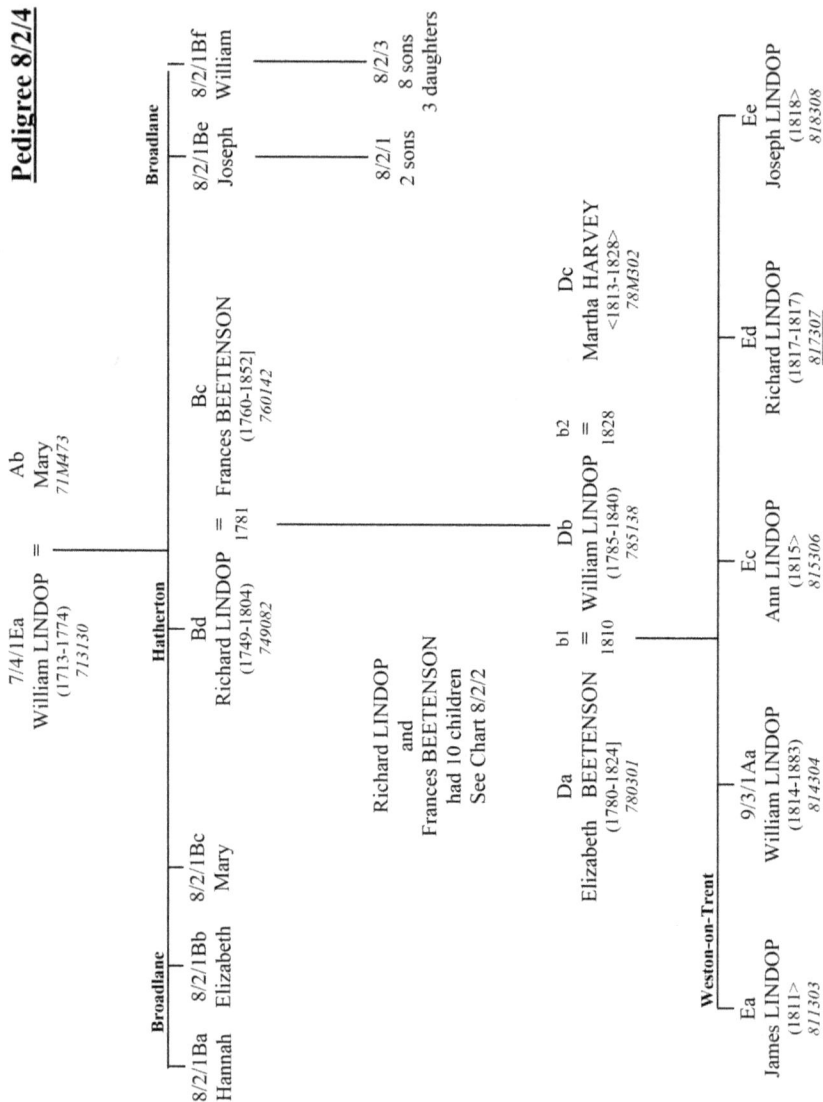

**Broadlane**

| 8/2/1Ba | 8/2/1Bb | 8/2/1Bc |
| Hannah | Elizabeth | Mary |

Ab
Mary
*71M473*

7/4/1Ea
William LINDOP
(1713-1774)
*713130*

=

**Broadlane**

| 8/2/1Be | 8/2/1Bf |
| Joseph | William |

8/2/1     8/2/3
2 sons    8 sons
        3 daughters

**Hatherton**

Bd
Richard LINDOP
(1749-1804)
*749082*
= 1781
Bc
Frances BEETENSON
(1760-1852]
*760142*

Richard LINDOP
and
Frances BEETENSON
had 10 children
See Chart 8/2/2

Da
Elizabeth BEETENSON
(1780-1824]
*780301*
b1 = 1810
Db
William LINDOP
(1785-1840)
*785138*
b2 = 1828
Dc
Martha HARVEY
<1813-1828>
*78M302*

**Weston-on-Trent**

Ea
James LINDOP
(1811>
*811303*

9/3/1Aa
William LINDOP
(1814-1883)
*814304*

Ec
Ann LINDOP
(1815>
*815306*

Ed
Richard LINDOP
(1817-1817)
*817307*

Ee
Joseph LINDOP
(1818>
*818308*

# Pedigree 8/2/5

Aa
Johannem PLANT = Margarettam HEMYS

Ab

**Broadlane**

7/4/1Dd
Richard LINDOP
(1678>
*678076*

Ba
Thomas
PLANT = Elizabeth
WATSON
(1730>

Bb

7/4/1Ee
William
LINDOP
(1713-1774)
*715130*

Bd
Mary
*71M473*

Ca
John
PLANT
(1757-1831)

Cb
Hannah
SILVESTER

Ce
Abraham
BARLOW ^1779 JOHNSON

Cf
Mary

8/2/2Bd
Richard LINDOP
(1749-1804)
*749082*

8/2/2Bc
Frances BEETENSON
(1760-1852)
*760142*

**Eccleshall**

Dd
Samuel
BARLOW
(1785-1815>
*785547*

d1
Ann
JACKSON
*78M1715*

Dg
Abraham
BARLOW
(1780>

Df
Edward
BARLOW
(1785>

De

Da
Mary PLANT = 
(1786-1851)
*786540*

Dc
Ann LINDOP
(1796-1815>
*796533*

**Eccleshall**

Db
Richard LINDOP
(1786-1832)
*786539*

d2
Ellen
BARLOW
(1816-1847>
*816548*

Ei

**Eccleshall**

**Pershall, near Eccleshall**

La
John

Eb
Thomas

Ec
Mary Ann

Ed
William

Ee
James

Ef
Caroline

Eg
Eliza

Eh
Richard
LINDOP
(1814-1847>
*814548*

Ef
Mary

Fg
Betsey

Eh
Abraham

Ei
Ann

# Pedigree 8/2/6

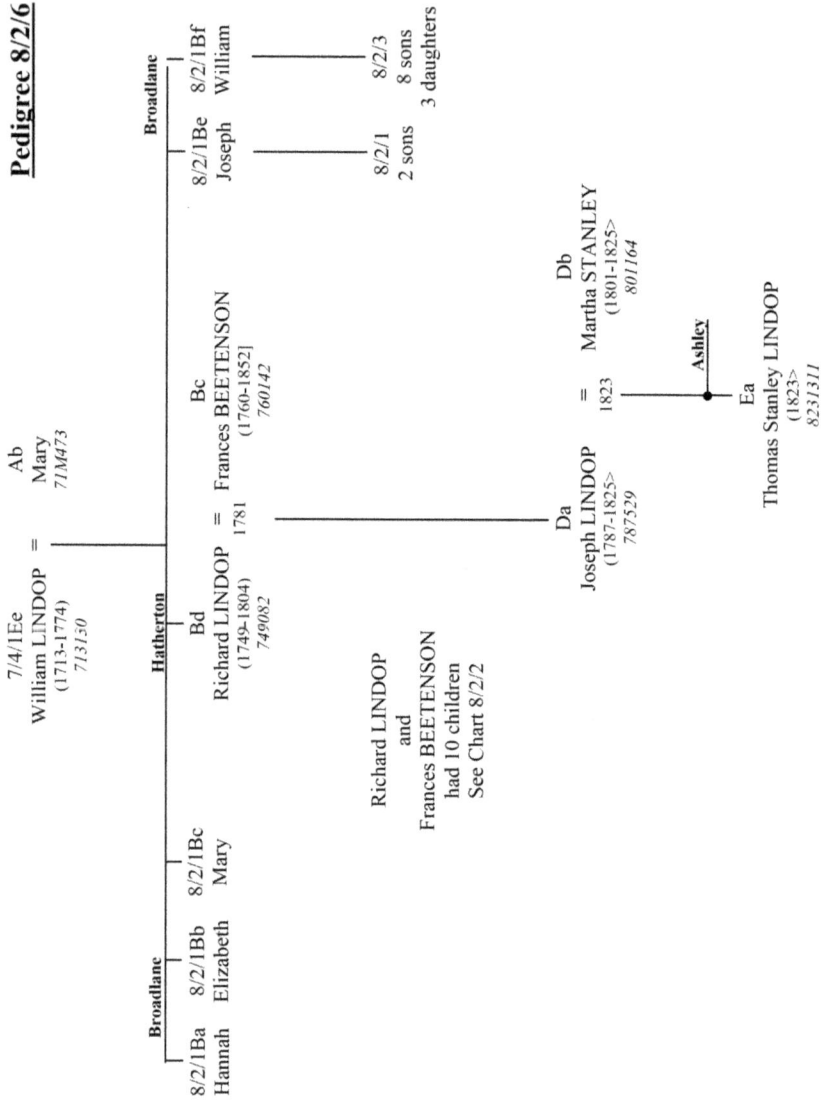

**Broadlane**

7/4/1Ee
William LINDOP = Ab
(1713-1774)    Mary
713150         71M473

**Broadlane**

8/2/1Ba    8/2/1Bb    8/2/1Bc
Hannah     Elizabeth   Mary

**Hatherton**

Bd                         Bc
Richard LINDOP  =  Frances BEETENSON
(1749-1804)    1781    (1760-1852]
749082                    760142

Richard LINDOP
and
Frances BEETENSON
had 10 children
See Chart 8/2/2

**Broadlane**

8/2/1Be    8/2/1Bf
Joseph     William

8/2/1      8/2/3
2 sons     8 sons
           3 daughters

Db
Martha STANLEY
(1801-1825>
801164

Da
Joseph LINDOP  =  1823
(1787-1825>
787529

**Ashley**

Ea
Thomas Stanley LINDOP
(1823>
823l3l1

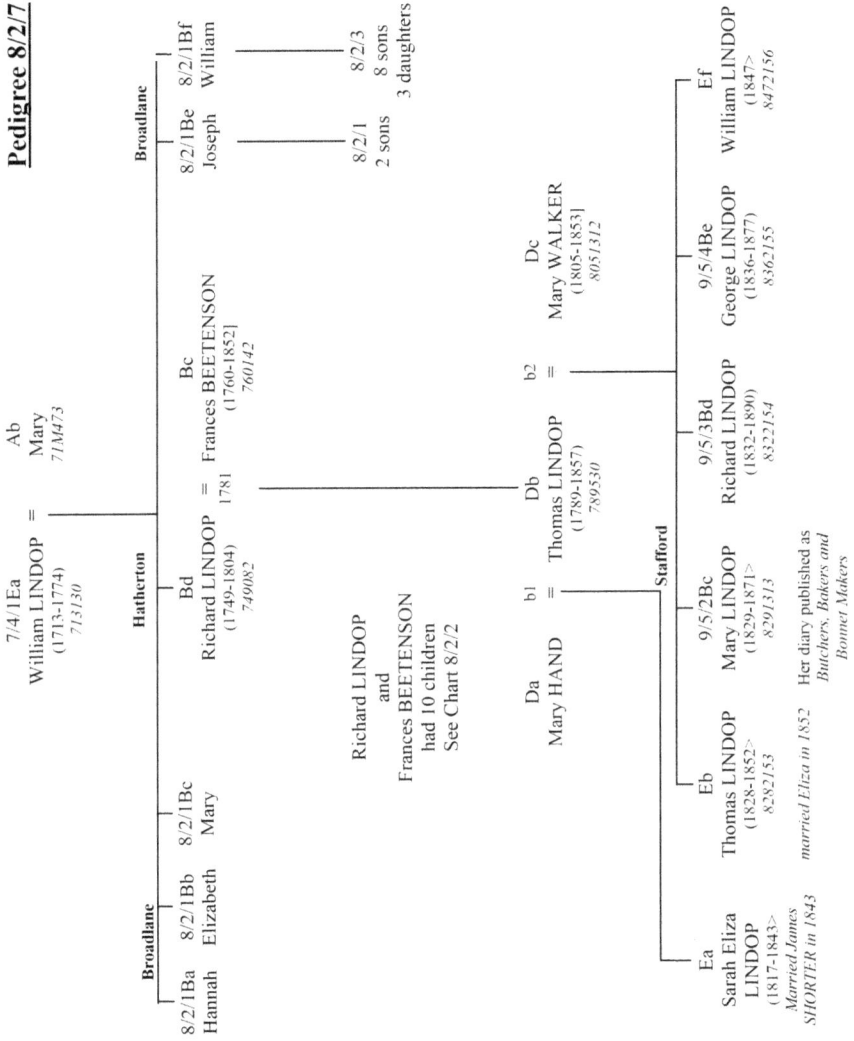

**Broadlane**

7/4/1Ea
William LINDOP
(1713-1774)
*713130*

Ab
Mary
*71M473*

8/2/1Ba
Hannah

8/2/1Bb
Elizabeth

8/2/1Bc
Mary

8/2/1Be
Joseph

8/2/1Bf
William

8/2/1
2 sons

8/2/3
8 sons
3 daughters

**Hatherton**

Bd
Richard LINDOP
(1749-1804)
*7490N2*

Bc
Frances BEETENSON
(1760-1852]
*760142*

= 1781

Richard LINDOP
and
Frances BEETENSON
had 10 children
See Chart 8/2/2

Da
Mary HAND

b1 =

Db
Thomas LINDOP
(1789-1857)
*789530*

b2 =

Dc
Mary WALKER
(1805-1853]
*805l312*

**Stafford**

Ea
Sarah Eliza
LINDOP
(1817-1843)
*Married James*
*SHORTER in 1843*

Eb
Thomas LINDOP
(1828-1852>
*8282l53*

9/5/2Bc
Mary LINDOP
(1829-1871>
*829l313*
*married Eliza in 1852*
*Her diary published as*
*Butchers, Bakers and*
*Bonnet Makers*

9/5/3Bd
Richard LINDOP
(1832-1890)
*8322l54*

9/5/4Be
George LINDOP
(1836-1877)
*8362l55*

Ef
William LINDOP
(1847>
*8472l56*

**Pedigree 8/2/8**

Broadlane

| 8/2/1Bc | 8/2/1Bf |
|---------|---------|
| Joseph | William |

8/2/1      8/2/3
2 sons     8 sons
         4 daughters

Ab
Mary
*71M473*

7/4/1Ea
William LINDOP
(1713-1774)
*713130*

=

**Broadlane**

| 8/2/1Ba | 8/2/1Bb | 8/2/1Bc |
|---------|---------|---------|
| Hannah | Elizabeth | Mary |

**Hatherton**

Bd
Richard LINDOP
(1749-1804)
*749082*

=
1781

Bc
Frances BEETENSON
(1760-1852]
*760142*

Richard LINDOP
and
Frances BEETENSON
had 10 children
See Chart 8/2/2

Da
John LINDOP
(1791-1842>
*79153/*

=

Db
Mary AUSTIN
<1810-1842>
*79M1315*

**Podmore**                    **Chatcull**

| Ea | Eb | Ec | Ed | Ee | Ef | Eg | Eh |
|----|----|----|----|----|----|----|----|
| Mary | John | Joseph | Ann | Elizabeth | Thomas | Caroline | Ellen |
| LINDOP | LINDOP | LINDOP | LINDOP | LINDOP | LINDOP | LINDOP | LINDOP |
| (1826< | (1828> | (1830> | (1832> | (1833> | (1835> | (1840> | (1842> |
| *826/316* | *828/317* | *830/318* | *832/319* | *833/320* | *835/321* | *840/322* | *842/323* |

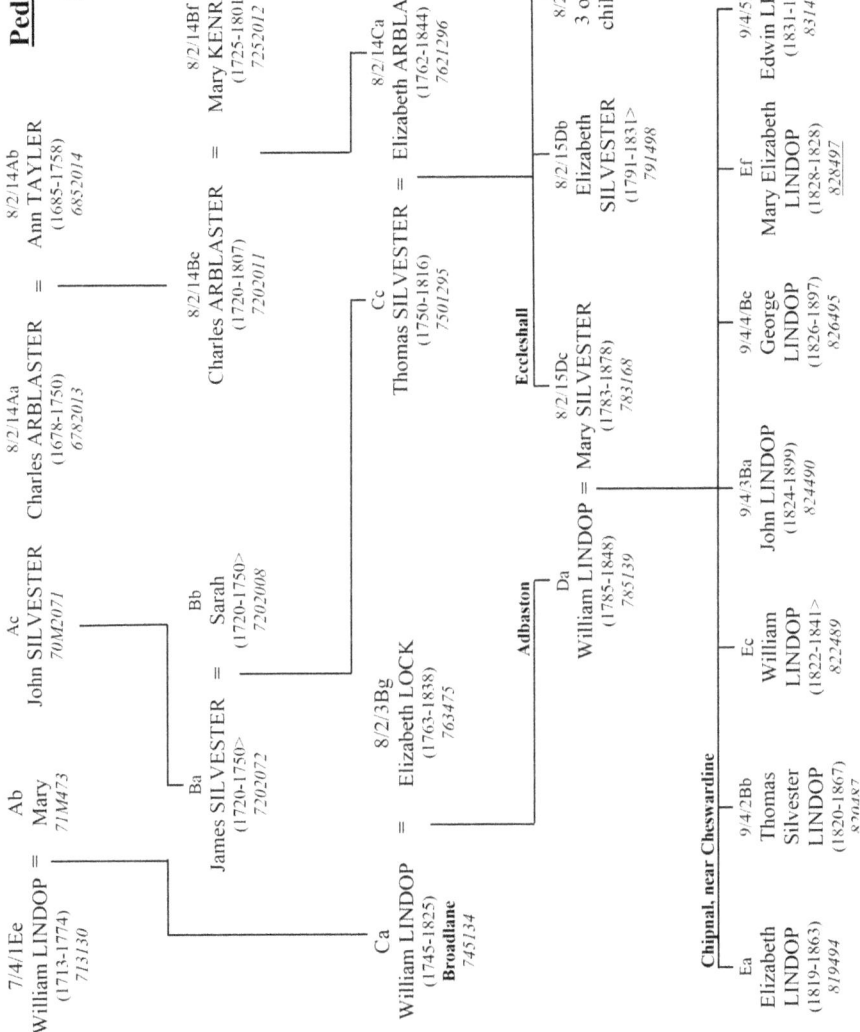

7/4/1Ee
William LINDOP
(1713-1774)
*713130*

Ab
Mary
*71M473*

Ac
John SILVESTER
*70M2071*

8/2/14Aa
Charles ARBLASTER
(1678-1750)
*6782013*

=

8/2/14Ab
Ann TAYLER
(1685-1758)
*6852014*

8/2/14Bc
Charles ARBLASTER
(1720-1807)
*7202011*

8/2/14Bf
Mary KENRICK
(1725-1801)
*7252012*

Bb
Sarah
(1720-1750>
*7202008*

Ba
James SILVESTER
(1720-1750>
*7202072*

=

Cc
Thomas SILVESTER
(1750-1816)
*7501295*

=

8/2/14Ca
Elizabeth ARBLASTER
(1762-1844)
*761296*

8/2/3Bg
Elizabeth LOCK
(1763-1838)
*763475*

=

Ca
William LINDOP
(1745-1825)
**Broadlane**
*745134*

**Adbaston**

Da
William LINDOP = Mary SILVESTER
(1785-1848)
*785139*

**Eccleshall**

8/2/15Dc
Mary SILVESTER
(1783-1878)
*783168*

8/2/15Db
Elizabeth
SILVESTER
(1791-1831>
*791498*

8/2/15
3 other
children

**Chipnal, near Cheswardine**

Ea
Elizabeth
LINDOP
(1819-1863)
*819494*

9/4/2Bb
Thomas
Silvester
LINDOP
(1820-1867)
*820467*

Ec
William
LINDOP
(1822-1841>
*822489*

9/4/3Ba
John LINDOP
(1824-1899)
*824490*

9/4/4Bc
George
LINDOP
(1826-1897)
*826495*

Ef
Mary Elizabeth
LINDOP
(1828-1828)
*828497*

9/4/5Bg
Edwin LINDOP
(1831-1901>
*831492*

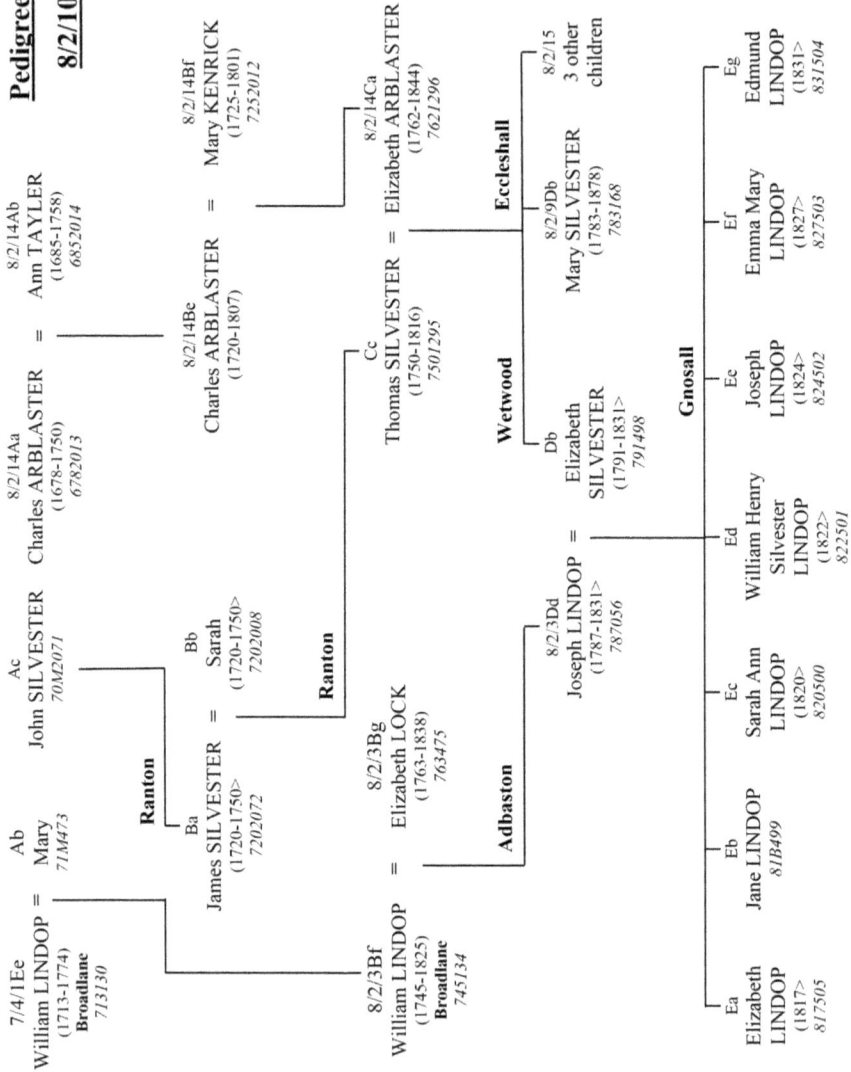

**Pedigree**

**8/2/10**

7/4/1Ee
William LINDOP =
(1713-1774)
**Broadlane**
713130

Ab
Mary
71M473

Ac
John SILVESTER
70M2071

8/2/14Aa
Charles ARBLASTER
(1678-1750)
6782013

8/2/14Ab
Ann TAYLER
(1685-1758)
6852014

8/2/14Bf
Mary KENRICK
(1725-1801)
7252012

**Ranton**

Ba
James SILVESTER =
(1720-1750▷)
7202072

Bb
Sarah
(1720-1750▷)
7202008

8/2/14Be
Charles ARBLASTER
(1720-1807)

**Ranton**

**Adbaston**

8/2/3Bf
William LINDOP =
(1745-1825)
**Broadlane**
745134

8/2/3Bg
Elizabeth LOCK
(1763-1838)
763475

Cc
Thomas SILVESTER =
(1750-1816)
7501295

8/2/14Ca
Elizabeth ARBLASTER
(1762-1844)
7621296

8/2/3Dd
Joseph LINDOP =
(1787-1831▷)
787056

Db
Elizabeth
SILVESTER
(1791-1831▷)
791498

**Wetwood**

**Eccleshall**

8/2/9Db
Mary SILVESTER
(1783-1878)
783168

8/2/15
3 other
children

**Gnosall**

Ea
Elizabeth
LINDOP
(1817▷)
817505

Eb
Jane LINDOP
81B499

Ec
Sarah Ann
LINDOP
(1820▷)
820500

Ed
William Henry
Silvester
LINDOP
(1822▷)
822501

Ee
Joseph
LINDOP
(1824▷)
824502

Ef
Emma Mary
LINDOP
(1827▷)
827503

Eg
Edmund
LINDOP
(1831▷)
831504

# Pedigree 8/2/11

To date I have found no connection between Samuel Whitefoot and Mary Elizabeth Whitefoot. It is possible that Samuel was christened on 7 August 1786 at Wistanstow the same Shropshire parish where Jemima was born. If so his father was Thomas Whitefoot and his mother Judith. Is this the same Thomas that later married Mary Pearks?

Bc
Thomas
WHITEFOOT
(1759>

Bd
Elizabeth
MINTON

Cd
Thomas
WHITEFOOT
(1782>

Ce
Mary
PEARKS
(1789>

7/4/1Dd
Richard LINDOP
(1678>
678076

8/2/3Ab
Mary
71M473

7/4/1Ee
William LINDOP
(1713-1774)
**Broadlane**
713130

8/2/3Bf
William
LINDOP
(1745-1825)
745134

8/2/3Bg
Elizabeth
LOCK
(1763-1838)
763475

Df
Jane
WHITEFOOT
(1813>
Married
Andrew WALKER

**Cardington**

De
Mary Elizabeth
WHITEFOOT
(1812-1871>
812171

**Adbaston**

Dc
John
LINDOP
(1792-1871)
792053

**High
Offley**

8/2/3
nine
other
children

Dd
Isaiah
LINDOP
(1805-1872)
805030

Ca
Richard GWILT

Cb
Ann

Db
Jemima GWELT
(1799-1841>
**Wistanstow**
799150

**Rushbury**

Ed
Jane LINDOP
(1836-1851>
836480

**Cardington**

Ee
Isaiah Whitefoot LINDOP
(1850-1871>
850482

Da
Samuel
WHITEFOOT
<1810-1824>
80M1758

cl 1823

Ea
Ann WHITEFOOT
(1824-1851>
**Eaton Heywood**
8241757

1829

Eb
John LINDOP
(1834-1841>
**Eaton Heywood**
8341655

9/6/1Ba
Edwin LINDOP
(1834-1871>
834481

1831

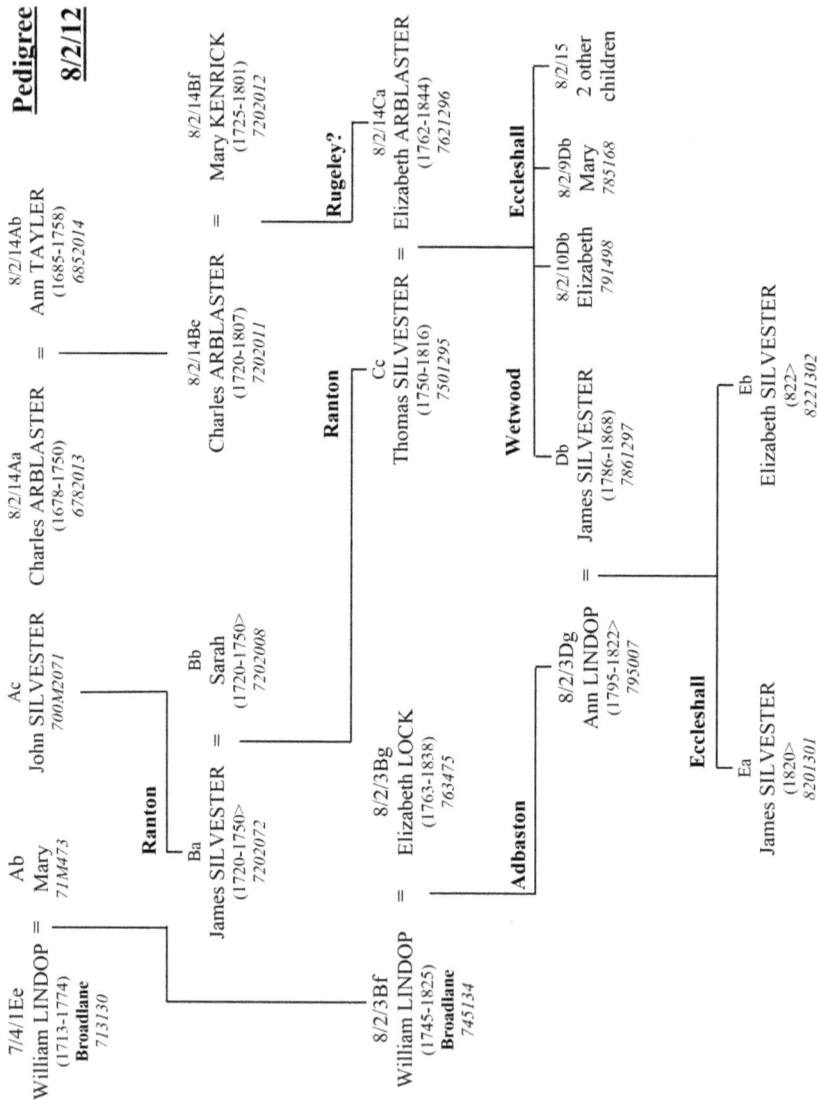

7/4/1Ee
William LINDOP =
(1713-1774)
**Broadlane**
*713130*

Ab
Mary
*71M473*

Ac
John SILVESTER
*700M2071*

8/2/14Aa
Charles ARBLASTER =
(1678-1750)
*6782013*

8/2/14Ab
Ann TAYLER
(1685-1758)
*6852014*

8/2/14Bf
Mary KENRICK
(1725-1801)
*7202012*

**Ranton**

Ba
James SILVESTER =
(1720-1750>
*7202072*

Bb
Sarah
(1720-1750>
*7202008*

8/2/14Be
Charles ARBLASTER
(1720-1807)
*7202011*

**Rugeley?**

8/2/14Ca
Elizabeth ARBLASTER
(1762-1844)
*7621296*

8/2/3Bf
William LINDOP
(1745-1825)
**Broadlane**
*745134*

8/2/3Bg
Elizabeth LOCK
(1763-1838)
*763475*

**Ranton**

Cc
Thomas SILVESTER =
(1750-1816)
*7501295*

**Adbaston**

=

8/2/3Dg
Ann LINDOP
(1795-1822>
*795007*

**Wetwood**

Db
James SILVESTER
(1786-1868)
*7861297*

8/2/10Db
Elizabeth
*791498*

**Eccleshall**

8/2/9Db
Mary
*785168*

8/2/15
2 other
children

=

**Eccleshall**

Ea
James SILVESTER
(1820>
*8201301*

Eb
Elizabeth SILVESTER
(822>
*8221302*

# Pedigree 8/2/13

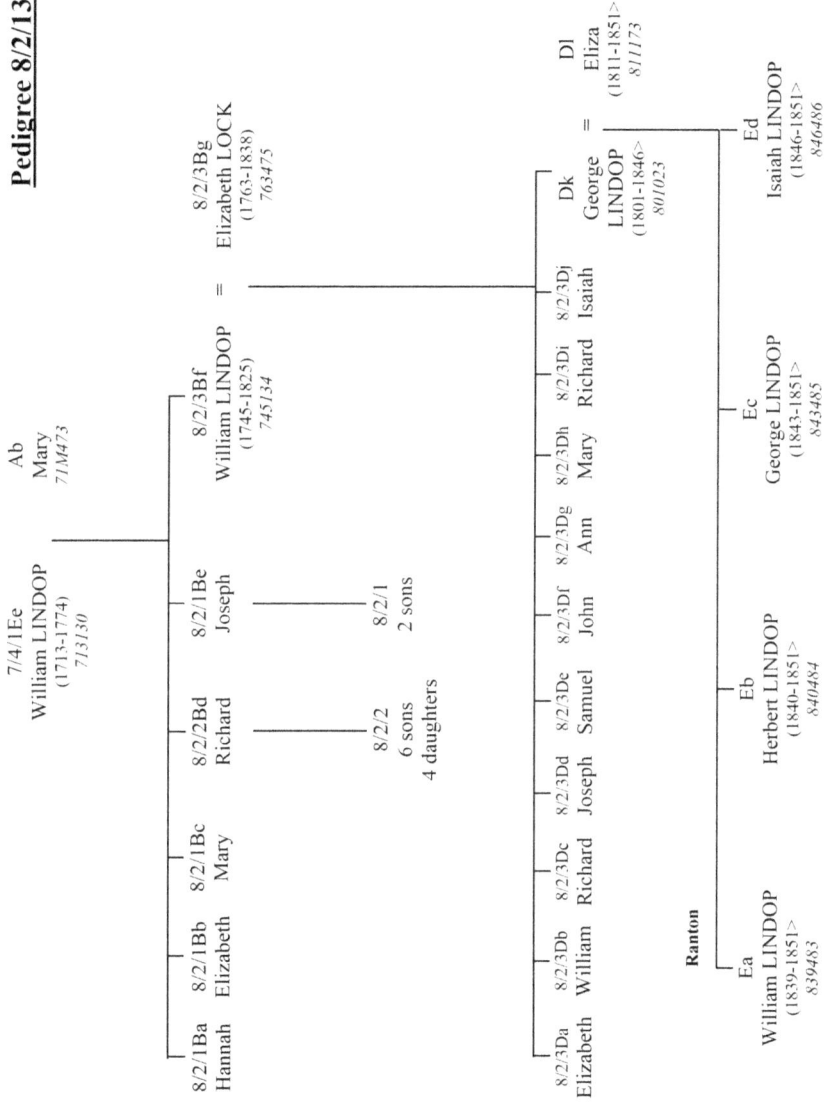

7/4/1Ee
William LINDOP
(1713-1774)
*713130*

Ab
Mary
*71M473*

=

8/2/3Bg
Elizabeth LOCK
(1763-1838)
*763475*

8/2/1Ba
Hannah

8/2/1Bb
Elizabeth

8/2/1Bc
Mary

8/2/2Bd
Richard

8/2/1Be
Joseph

8/2/3Bf
William LINDOP
(1745-1825)
*745134*

8/2/2
6 sons
4 daughters

8/2/1
2 sons

Dk
George
LINDOP
(1801-1846>
*801023*

Dl
Eliza
(1811-1851>
*811173*

=

8/2/3Da
Elizabeth

8/2/3Db
William

8/2/3Dc
Richard

8/2/3Dd
Joseph

8/2/3De
Samuel

8/2/3Df
John

8/2/3Dg
Ann

8/2/3Dh
Mary

8/2/3Di
Richard

8/2/3Dj
Isaiah

Ed
Isaiah LINDOP
(1846-1851>
*846486*

**Ranton**

Ea
William LINDOP
(1839-1851>
*839483*

Eb
Herbert LINDOP
(1840-1851>
*840484*

Ec
George LINDOP
(1843-1851>
*843485*

# Pedigree 8/2/14

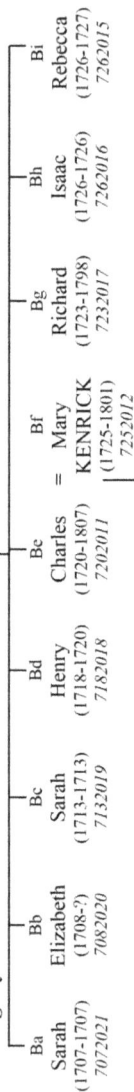
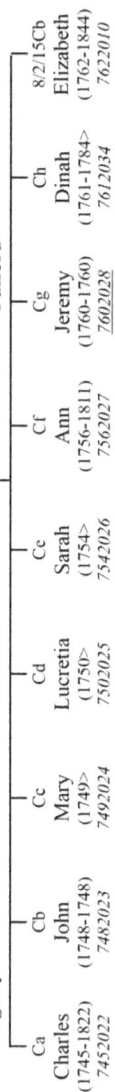
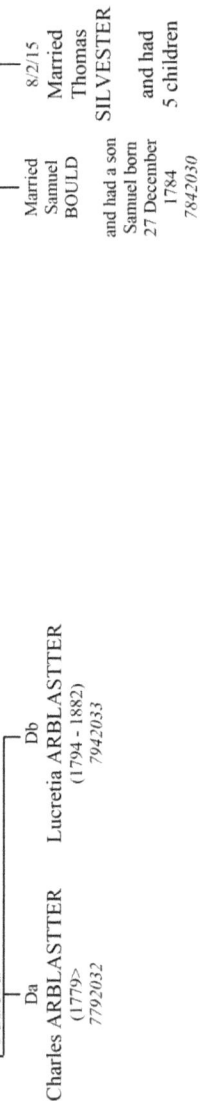

Aa
Charles ARBLASTER
(1678-1750)
6782013

=

Ab
Ann TAYLER
(1685-1758)
6852014

**Rugeley**

Ba
Sarah
(1707-1707)
7072021

Bb
Elizabeth
(1708-?)
7082020

Bc
Sarah
(1713-1713)
7132019

Bd
Henry
(1718-1720)
7182018

Be
Charles
(1720-1807)
7202011

Bf
= Mary
KENRICK
(1725-1801)
7252012

Bg
Richard
(1723-1798)
7232017

Bh
Isaac
(1726-1726)
7262016

Bi
Rebecca
(1726-1727)
7262015

**Rugeley**

**Colwich**

**Fulford**

Ca
Charles
(1745-1822)
7452022

= Ann TABBERNOR (1755-1788)
7552031

Cb
John
(1748-1748)
7482023

Cc
Mary
(1749>)
7492024

Cd
Lucretia
(1750>)
7502025

Ce
Sarah
(1754>)
7542026

Cf
Ann
(1756-1811)
7562027

Cg
Jeremy
(1760-1760)
7602028

Ch
Dinah
(1761-1784>)
7612034

8/2/15Cb
Elizabeth
(1762-1844)
7622010

**Fulford**

Da
Charles ARBLASTTER
(1779>)
7792032

Db
Lucretia ARBLASTTER
(1794 - 1882)
7942033

Married
Samuel
BOULD
and had a son
Samuel born
27 December
1784
7842030

8/2/15
Married
Thomas
SILVESTER
and had
5 children

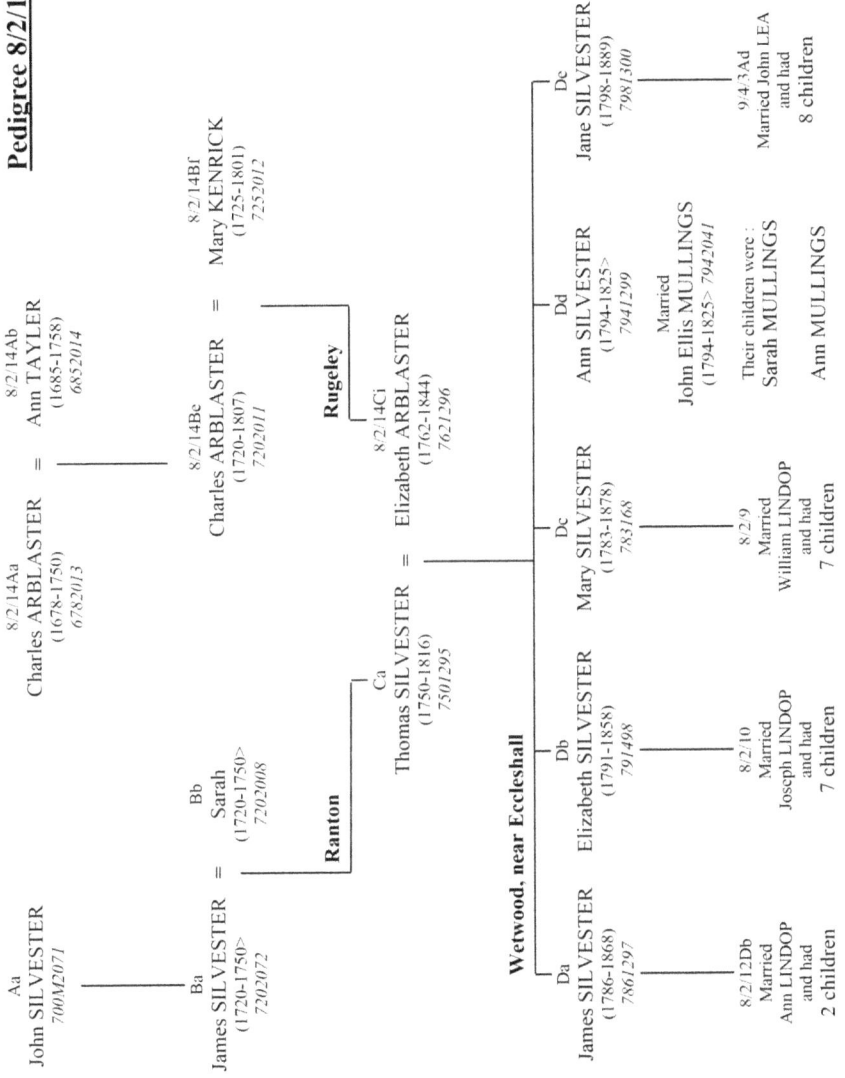

Aa
John SILVESTER
*700M207I*

Ba
James SILVESTER
(1720-1750>
*7202072*

=

Bb
Sarah
(1720-1750>
*7202008*

**Ranton**

8/2/14Aa
Charles ARBLASTER
(1678-1750)
*678203*

=

8/2/14Ab
Ann TAYLER
(1685-1758)
*6852014*

8/2/14Bc
Charles ARBLASTER
(1720-1807)
*720201I*

=

8/2/14Bf
Mary KENRICK
(1725-1801)
*725201I2*

Ca
Thomas SILVESTER
(1750-1816)
*750I295*

=

8/2/14Ci
Elizabeth ARBLASTER
(1762-1844)
*762I296*

**Rugeley**

**Wetwood, near Eccleshall**

Da
James SILVESTER
(1786-1868)
*786I297*

8/2/12Db
Married
Ann LINDOP
and had
2 children

Db
Elizabeth SILVESTER
(1791-1858)
*791I498*

8/2/10
Married
Joseph LINDOP
and had
7 children

Dc
Mary SILVESTER
(1783-1878)
*783I68*

8/2/9
Married
William LINDOP
and had
7 children

Dd
Ann SILVESTER
(1794-1825>
*794I299*

Married
John Ellis MULLINGS
(1794-1825> *794204I*

Their children were :
Sarah MULLINGS

Ann MULLINGS

De
Jane SILVESTER
(1798-1889)
*798I300*

9/4/3Ad
Married John LEA
and had
8 children

Checkley

Bg
Ann CORKE
(1753>
75I1597

Ad
Elizabeth
74M1596

Ac
Thomas CORKE
74M1595

=

Bf
Betty LINDOP
<1757]
75B290

Be
Richard
LINDOP
[1752-1805]
752289

Bd
Elizabeth
CORKE
[1763-1838]
763288

7/4/2Ec
William LINDOP   =   Mary ROWSON
(1713-1774)      1739   (1715-1752>
713282                   715283

**Wybunbury**

Bc
William
LINDOP
[1745-1825]
745287

=   1782

Bb
Mary LINDOP
(1743>
743286

Ba
Hannah
LINDOP
(1739>
739285

**Adbaston**

Da
Elizabeth
LINDOP
[1783>
783291

Db
Richard
LINDOP
[1785>
785292

Dc
Joseph
LINDOP
[1787>
787293

Dd
Samuel
LINDOP
[1789>
789294

De
John
LINDOP
[1792-1857]
792295

Df
Ann
LINDOP
[1795>
795296

Dg
Mary
LINDOP
[1797>
797297

Dh
George
LINDOP
(1800?>
79B298

Di
Richard
LINDOP
[1801>
801299

Dj
Issiah
LINDOP
[1805>
805300

Aa
Hannah
(<1730)
*71M697*

=

*7/5/5Dh*
Thomas LINDOP
(1699-1748)
*699724*

=

*7/5/5Di*
Rebehak WRIGHT
(1702-1773)
*7021803*

**Clutton**

Ba
Mary
LINDOP
(1730-
1773)
*730698*

Bb
Rebecca
LINDOP
(1732-
1745>
Married
Charles
JONES

Bc
Anne
LINDOP
(1733>
*7331806*

Bd
Samuel
LINDOP
(1735>
*7351807*

Be
Thomas
LINDOP
(1735>
*7351808*

Bf
William
LINDOP
(1737>
*7371809*

Bg
Benjamin
LINDOP
(1738-1741)
*7381810*

Bh
Peter
LINDOP
(1740-1741)
*7401811*

Bi
Joseph
LINDOP
(1743-1826)
*743641*
Married
Martha
THELWELL
2 March 1770

Bj
Joshua
LINDOP
(1744-1826)
*7441813*

Bk
Benjamin
LINDOP
(1747)
*7471814*

**Hampton**

Da
Mary LINDOP
(1773-1790)
*773643*

Db
Martha LINDOP
(1777-1822)
*777644*

Dc
Joseph LINDOP
(1777-1822)
*777645*

Peter WRIGHT
(1670-1742)
*6701816*

=

Rebecca POYNTON
(1670-1731)
*6701817*

John LARDEN
(<1710-1726)
*70M1N15*

1723

=

Rebehak WRIGHT
(1702-1773)
*7021803*

=

Thomas LINDOP
(1699-1748)
*699724*

John LARDEN
(1724-1791)
*7241818*

See above

This is rather a complex chart because
both Thomas and Rebehak (Rebecca)
had both married previously and had
children by their first marriages.

## Pedigree 8/5/1

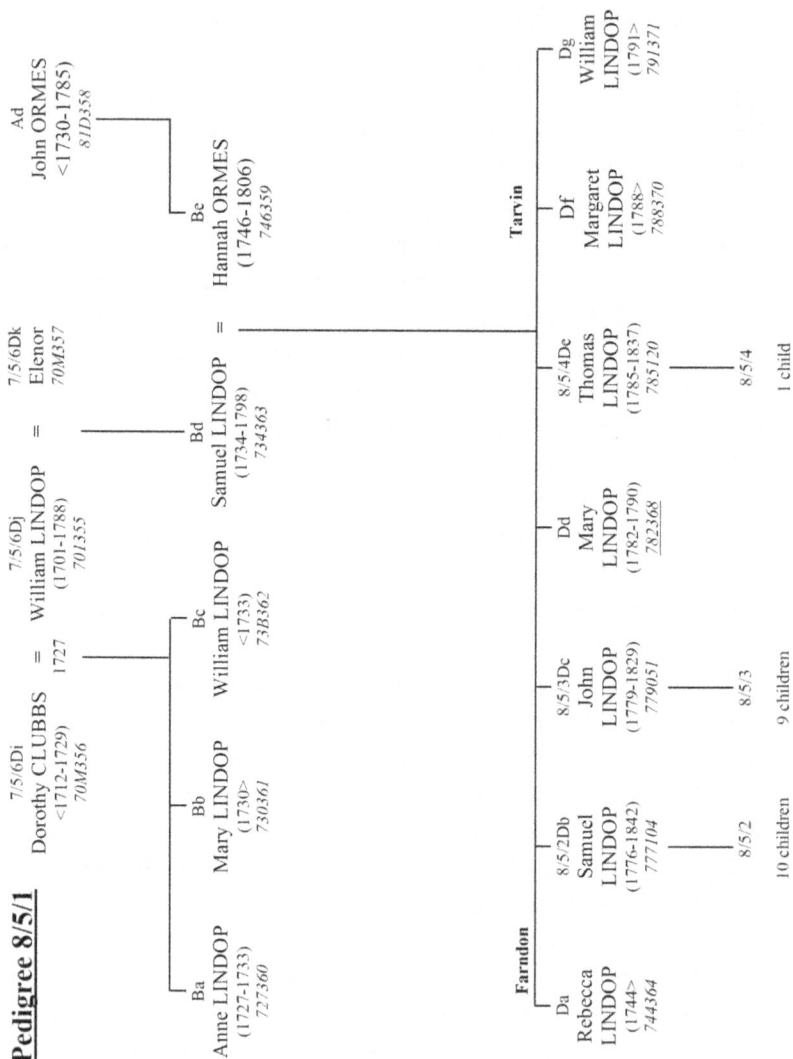

**Ad**
John ORMES
<1730-1785)
*81D358*

**Be**
Hannah ORMES
(1746-1806)
*746359*

**7/5/6Di**
Dorothy CLUBBS
<1712-1729)
*70M356*

=
1727

**7/5/6Dj**
William LINDOP
(1701-1788)
*701355*

=

**7/5/6Dk**
Elenor
*70M357*

**Ba**
Anne LINDOP
(1727-1733)
*727360*

**Bb**
Mary LINDOP
(1730>
*730361*

**Bc**
William LINDOP
<1733)
*73B362*

**Bd**
Samuel LINDOP
(1734-1798)
*734363*

=

**Farndon**

**Da**
Rebecca
LINDOP
(1744>
*744364*

**Tarvin**

**Dg**
William
LINDOP
(1791>
*791371*

**Df**
Margaret
LINDOP
(1788>
*788370*

**8/5/4De**
Thomas
LINDOP
(1785-1837)
*785120*

**Dd**
Mary
LINDOP
(1782-1790)
*782368*

**8/5/3Dc**
John
LINDOP
(1779-1829)
*779051*

**8/5/2Db**
Samuel
LINDOP
(1776-1842)
*777104*

8/5/4
1 child

8/5/3
9 children

8/5/2
10 children

# Pedigree 8/5/2

Ad
John ORMES
<1730-1785)
*81D358*

Be
Hannah ORMES
(1746-1806)
*746359*

7.5.6Di
Dorothy CLUBBS
<1712-1729)
*70M356*

=
1727

7.5.6Dj
William LINDOP
(1701-1788)
*701355*

=

7.5.6Dk
Elenor
*70M357*

Ba
Anne LINDOP
(1727-1733)
*727360*

Bb
Mary LINDOP
(1730>
*730361*

Bc
William LINDOP
<1733)
*73B362*

Bd
Samuel LINDOP
(1734-1798)
*734363*

**Farndon**

8.5.1Db
Samuel LINDOP
(1776-1842)
*777104*
*777365*

=

Dc
Mary EVANS
(1784-1842)
*784145*

**Tarvin**

8.5.1Da
Rebecca

Ea
Samuel
LINDOP
(1810-1885)
*810372*

Eb
William
LINDOP
(1812>
*812374*

Ec
Thomas
LINDOP
(1813>
*813375*

Ed
John
LINDOP
(1816-1895)
*816376*

Ee
Mary
LINDOP
(1818-1822)
*818377*

Ef
Richard
LINDOP
(1820>
*820378*

8.5.1Dc
John

8.5.1Dc
Thomas

8.5.1Dd
Mary

Eg
Margaret
LINDOP
(1821-1850>
*821379*

8.5.1De
Thomas

Eh
Joseph
LINDOP
(1823-1878)
*823380*

8.5.1Df
Margaret

Ei
Mary Ann
LINDOP
(1825-1842)
*825381*

8.5.1Dg
William

Ej
Edwin
LINDOP
(1829-1829)
*828382*

This chart is discussed in more
detail in *Lindop: A Family History*
by John Barford Lindop
published by Mercianotes.
(ISBN: 9781522882947 )

# Pedigree 8/5/3

Ad
John ORMES
<1730-1785>
81D358

Be
Hannah ORMES
(1746-1806)
746359

7:5:6Di
Dorothy CLUBBS
<1712-1729>
70M356

=
1727

7:5:6Dj
William LINDOP
(1701-1788)
701355

=

7:5:6Dk
Elenor
70M357

Bd
Samuel LINDOP
(1734-1798)
734363

=

Ba
Anne LINDOP
(1727-1733)
727360

Bb
Mary LINDOP
(1730>
730361

Bc
William LINDOP
<1733)
73B362

**Farndon**

8:5:1Da
Rebecca

8:5:1Db
Samuel

8:5:1Dc
John LINDOP
(1779-1829)
779051

=

Dd
Mary HUGHES
<1794-1828>
77M176

**Tarvin**

8:5:1Dd
Mary

8:5:1De
Thomas

8:5:1Df
Margaret

8:5:1Dg
William

**Chester**

Ea
Margaret
LINDOP
(1810>
810060

Eb
John
LINDOP
(1811>
811910

Ec
William
LINDOP
(1813-1844>
813140

Ed
Charles
LINDOP
(1815-1859>
815009

Ee
Thomas
LINDOP
(1817>
817122

Ef
Samuel
LINDOP
(1819>
819911

Eg
George
LINDOP
(1822>
822024

Ei
Ei
John Arthur
LINDOP
(1827>
828913

Eh
Philip Henry
LINDOP
(1824>
824912

# Pedigree 8/5/4

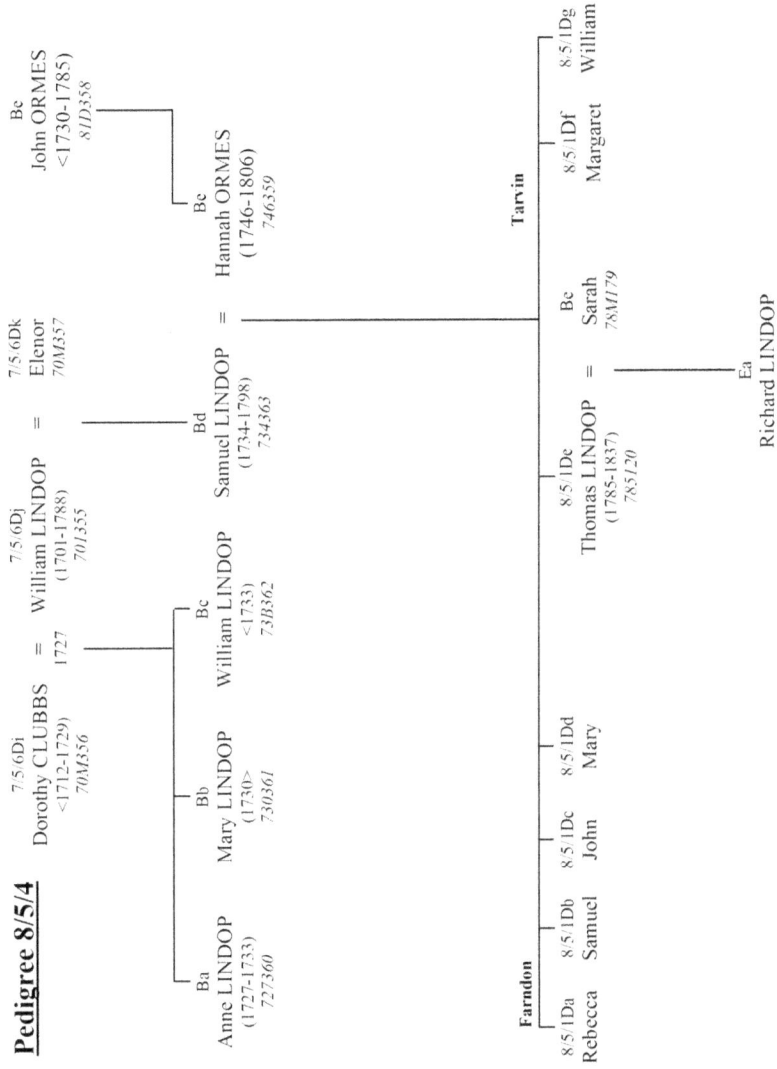

Ba
Anne LINDOP
(1727-1733)
727360

7.5.6Di
Dorothy CLUBBS    =
<1712-1729)       1727
70M356

7.5.6Dj
William LINDOP
(1701-1788)
70J355

7.5.6Dk
=   Elenor
    70M357

Bb
Mary LINDOP
(1730>
730361

Bc
William LINDOP
<1733)
73B362

Bd
Samuel LINDOP
(1734-1798)
734363

Bc
John ORMES
<1730-1785)
81D358

Bc
Hannah ORMES
(1746-1806)
746359

=

**Farndon**

8/5/1Da
Rebecca

8/5/1Db
Samuel

8/5/1Dc
John

8/5/1Dd
Mary

8/5/1De
Thomas LINDOP
(1785-1837)
785J20

Bc
Sarah
78M179

**Tarvin**

8/5/1Df
Margaret

8/5/1Dg
William

Ea
=   Richard LINDOP

7/4/2De
Thomas LINDOP
<1698-1734>
69M1430

=

Ab
Mary
<1700-1736>
69M1431

Aa
John BADDELEY
(1670-1754)
6701433

=

Ab
Elizabeth
<1720-1762>
67M1434

Ba
John LINDOP
(1712-1771)
7121429

=

Bb
Elizabeth BADDELEY
<1720-1745>
71M21432

It is thought that the Mary who married
Thomas was Mary Eyreboth and the John
born 1712 was their third child. Their second,
also John was born and died in 1709, but
there is no proof for this hypothesis

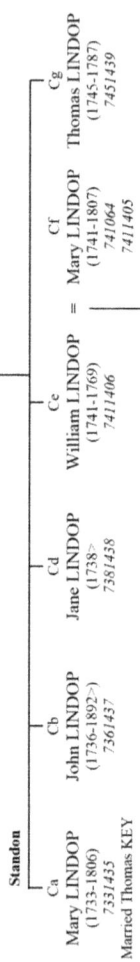

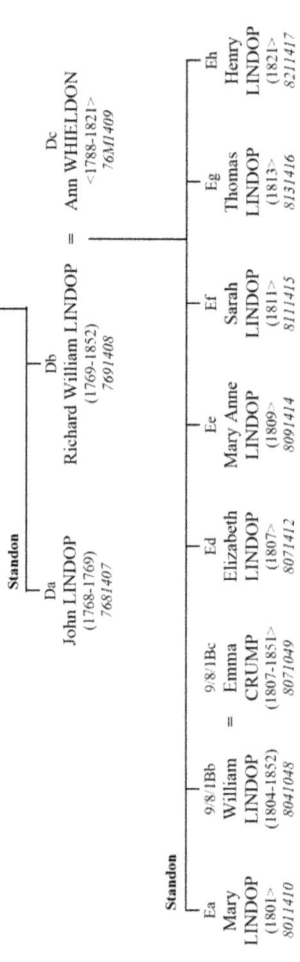

**Standon**

Ca
Mary LINDOP
(1733-1806)
7331435
Married Thomas KEY

Cb
John LINDOP
(1736-1892>
7361437

Cd
Jane LINDOP
(1738>
7381438

Ce
William LINDOP
(1741-1769)
7411406

=

Cf
Mary LINDOP
(1741-1807)
741064
7411405

Cg
Thomas LINDOP
(1745-1787)
7451439

**Standon**

Da
John LINDOP
(1768-1769)
7681407

Db
Richard William LINDOP
(1769-1852)
7691408

=

Dc
Ann WHIELDON
<1788-1821>
76M1409

**Standon**

Ea
Mary
LINDOP
(1801>
8011410

9/8/1Bb
William
LINDOP
(1804-1852)
8041048

=

9/8/1Bc
Emma
CRUMP
(1807-1851>
8071049

Ed
Elizabeth
LINDOP
(1807>
8071412

Ee
Mary Anne
LINDOP
(1809>
8091414

Ef
Sarah
LINDOP
(1811>
8111415

Eg
Thomas
LINDOP
(1813>
8131416

Eh
Henry
LINDOP
(182l>
8211417

# Pedigree 8/6/2

7/4/2De
Thomas & Mary
LINDOP

8/6/1Ab
John & Elizabeth
BADDELEY

Ab
Debora NEWALL
<1692-1708>
68M160
= 1704
7/4/2De
Robert LINDOP
of Barthomley
68M096

Bb
Elizabeth Meakin
<1720-1745>
72M175

Ba
John LINDOP
(1712-1771)
712/429

Bb
Elizabeth BADDELEY
<1720-1745>
71M/432

Ba
Thomas LINDOP
<1707>
70B/119

Ba
Richard LINDOP
<1708-1767>
72M081
= 1729

Cg
William LINDOP
(1742-1767>
742/31

Ce

Cf
Mary LINDOP
(1741-1807)
741/064

Cg
Richard LINDOP
(1733>
733/170

Cg
John LINDOP
(1739>
739/049

Cg
Hannah LINDOP
(1739>
739/027

William LINDOP
(1741-1769)
741/406
=
Mary LINDOP

Db
Richard William LINDOP
(1769-1852)
769/408

Dc
Ann WHEELDON
<1788-1821>
76M/409
=

**Standon**
Da
John LINDOP
(1768-1769)
768/407

**Standon**
Ea
Mary
LINDOP
(1801>
801/410

9/8/1Bb
William
LINDOP
(1804-1852)
804/048
=
9/8/1Bc
Emma
CRUMP
(1807-1851>
807/049

Ed
Elizabeth
LINDOP
(1807>
807/412

Ee
Mary Anne
LINDOP
(1809>
809/414

Ef
Sarah
LINDOP
(1811>
811/415

Eg
Thomas
LINDOP
(1813>
813/416

Eh
Henry
LINDOP
(1821>
821/417

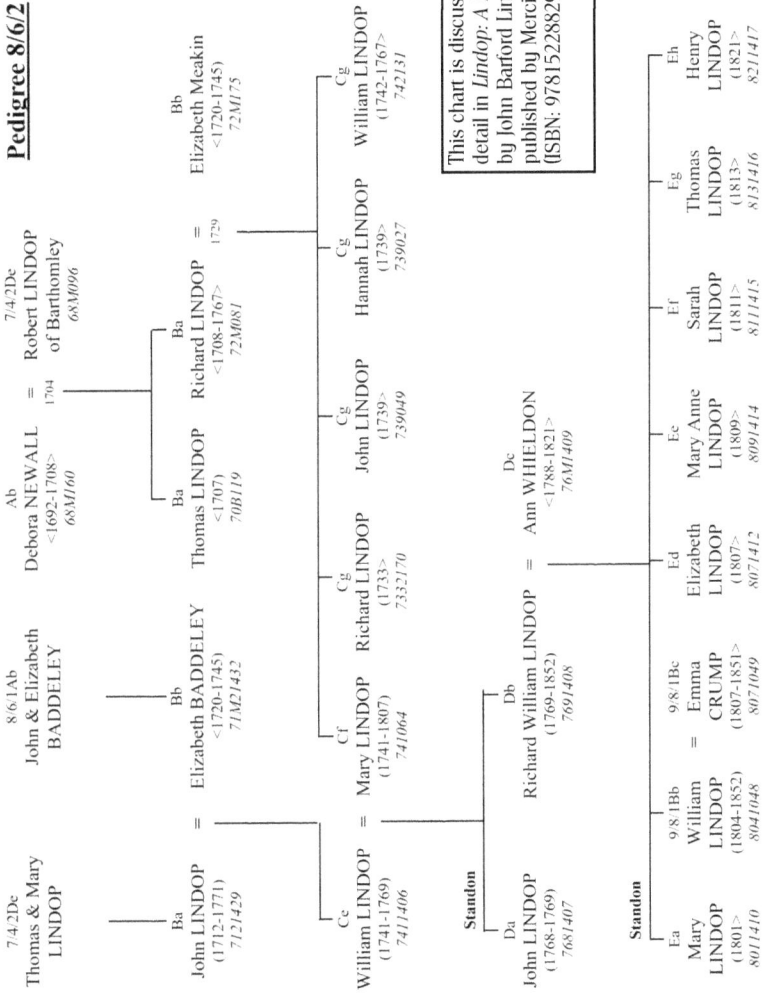

This chart is discussed in more
detail in *Lindop: A Family History*
by John Barford Lindop
published by Mercianotes.
(ISBN: 9781522882947 )

# Pedigree 8/6/3

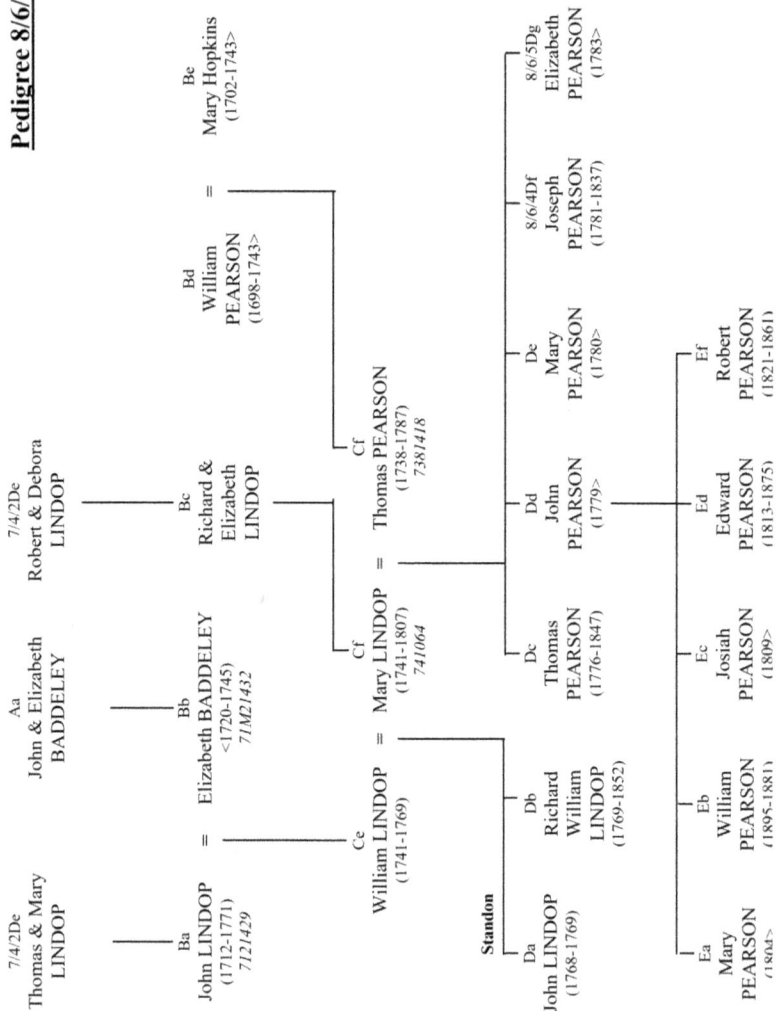

7/4/2De
Thomas & Mary
LINDOP

Aa
John & Elizabeth
BADDELEY

7/4/2De
Robert & Debora
LINDOP

Be
Mary Hopkins
(1702-1743>

Ba
John LINDOP
(1712-1771)
*7121429*

Bb
Elizabeth BADDELEY
<1720-1745)
*71M21432*

Bc
Richard &
Elizabeth
LINDOP

Bd
William
PEARSON
(1698-1743>

=

William LINDOP = Elizabeth BADDELEY
(1741-1769)

Ce

Cf
Mary LINDOP
(1741-1807)
*741064*

=

Cf
Thomas PEARSON
(1738-1787)
*7381418*

**Standon**

Da
John LINDOP
(1768-1769)

Db
Richard
William
LINDOP
(1769-1852)

Dc
Thomas
PEARSON
(1776-1847)

Dd
John
PEARSON
(1779>

De
Mary
PEARSON
(1780>

8/6/4Df
Joseph
PEARSON
(1781-1837)

8/6/5Dg
Elizabeth
PEARSON
(1783>

Ea
Mary
PEARSON
(1804>

Eb
William
PEARSON
(1805-1881)

Ec
Josiah
PEARSON
(1809>

Ed
Edward
PEARSON
(1813-1875)

Ef
Robert
PEARSON
(1821-1861)

# Pedigree 8/6/4

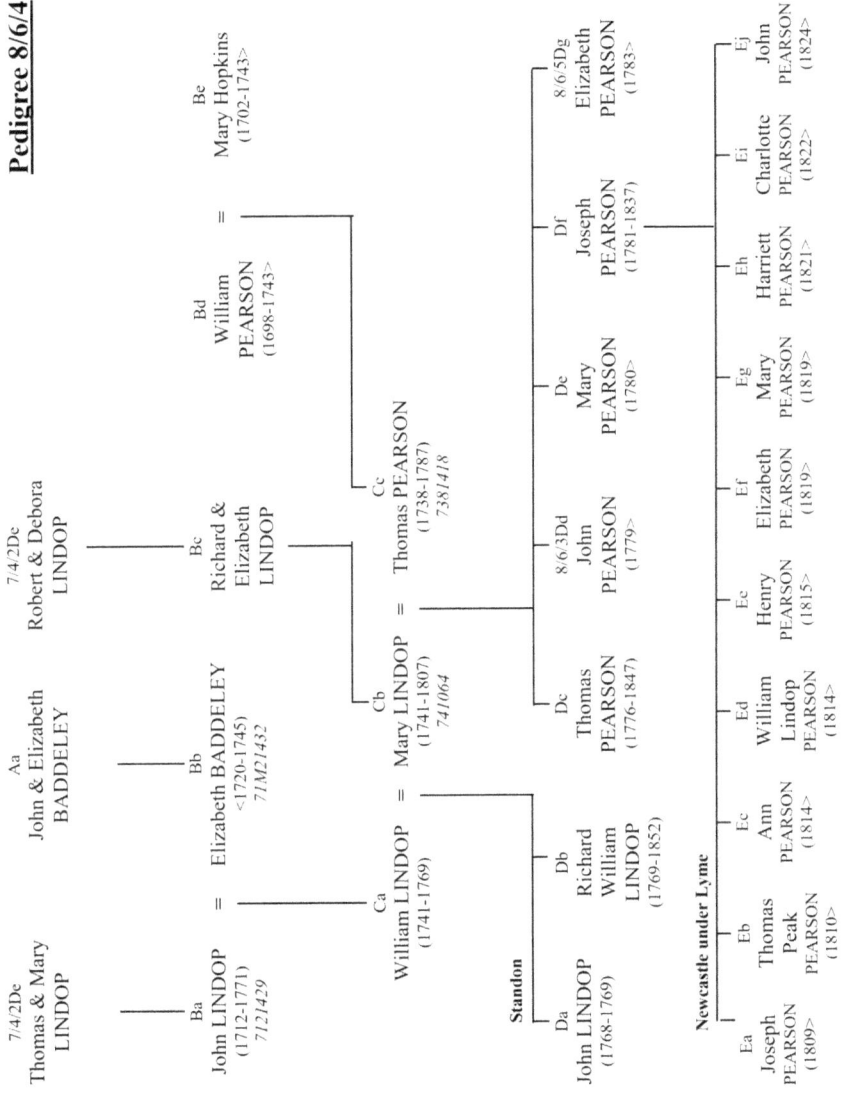

7/4/2De
Thomas & Mary
LINDOP

Ba
John LINDOP
(1712-1771)
*7121429*

Aa
John & Elizabeth
BADDELEY

Bb
Elizabeth BADDELEY
<1720-1745>
*71M21432*

7/4/2De
Robert & Debora
LINDOP

Bc
Richard &
Elizabeth
LINDOP

Bd
William
PEARSON
(1698-1743>

=

Be
Mary Hopkins
(1702-1743>

Ca
William LINDOP
(1741-1769)

=

Cb
Mary LINDOP
(1741-1807)
*741064*

Cc
Thomas PEARSON
(1738-1787)
*738/4/8*

**Standon**

Db
Richard
William
LINDOP
(1769-1852)

Dc
Thomas
PEARSON
(1776-1847)

Dd
8/6/3
John
PEARSON
(1779>

De
Mary
PEARSON
(1780>

Df
Joseph
PEARSON
(1781-1837)

Dg
8/6/5
Elizabeth
PEARSON
(1783>

Da
John LINDOP
(1768-1769)

**Newcastle under Lyme**

Ea
Joseph
PEARSON
(1809>

Eb
Thomas
Peak
PEARSON
(1810>

Ec
Ann
PEARSON
(1814>

Ed
William
Lindop
PEARSON
(1814>

Ec
Henry
PEARSON
(1815>

Ef
Elizabeth
PEARSON
(1819>

Eg
Mary
PEARSON
(1819>

Eh
Harriett
PEARSON
(1821>

Ei
Charlotte
PEARSON
(1822>

Ej
John
PEARSON
(1824>

# Pedigree 8/6/5

7/4/2De
Thomas & Mary LINDOP

Aa
John & Elizabeth BADDELEY

7/4/2De
Robert & Debora LINDOP

Be
Mary Hopkins
(1702-1743>

Bd
William PEARSON
(1698-1743>

=

Ba
John LINDOP
(1712-1771)
7121429

Bb
Elizabeth BADDELEY
<1720-1745)
71M21432

Bc
Richard & Elizabeth LINDOP

=

Ca
William LINDOP
(1741-1769)

=

Cb
Mary LINDOP
(1741-1807)
741064

=

Cc
Thomas PEARSON
(1738-1787)
7381418

**Standon**

Da
John LINDOP
(1768-1769)

Db
Richard William LINDOP
(1769-1852)

Dc
Thomas PEARSON
(1776-1847)

Dd
John PEARSON
(1779>

De
Mary PEARSON
(1780>

Df
Joseph PEARSON
(1781-1837)

Dg
Elizabeth PEARSON
(1783>

=

Dh
Thomas MOSS

**Eccleshall**

Ea
William MOSS
(1801>

Eb
Martha MOSS
(1803>

Ec
Mary MOSS
(1805>

Ed
Thomas Pearson MOSS
(1806-1880>

Ee
Elizabeth MOSS
(1808>

Ef
John MOSS
(1810-1867>

# Part 4

# 19<sup>th</sup> Century

# Pedigree 9/1/1

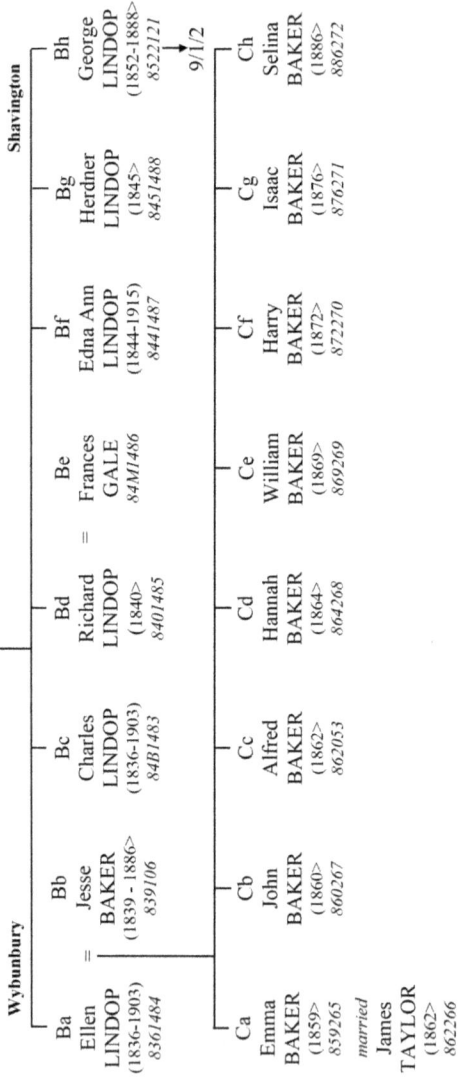

**Shavington**

8/1/3Df
Thomas LINDOP
[1801-1869]
*8011479*

Ab
Sarah MOSTON
(1804-1871)
*8041480*

=

**Wybunbury**

Ba
Ellen
LINDOP
(1836-1903)
*8361484*

=

Bb
Jesse
BAKER
(1839 - 1886>
*839106*

Bc
Charles
LINDOP
(1836-1903)
*84B1483*

Bd
Richard
LINDOP
(1840>
*8401485*

=

Be
Frances
GALE
*84M1486*

Bf
Edna Ann
LINDOP
(1844-1915)
*8441487*

Bg
Herdner
LINDOP
(1845>
*8451488*

Bh
George
LINDOP
(1852-1888>
*8522121*

→ 9/1/2

Ca
Emma
BAKER
(1859>
*859265*
*married*
James
TAYLOR
(1862>
*862266*

Cb
John
BAKER
(1860>
*860267*

Cc
Alfred
BAKER
(1862>
*862053*

Cd
Hannah
BAKER
(1864>
*864268*

Ce
William
BAKER
(1869>
*869269*

Cf
Harry
BAKER
(1872>
*872270*

Cg
Isaac
BAKER
(1876>
*876271*

Ch
Selina
BAKER
(1886>
*886272*

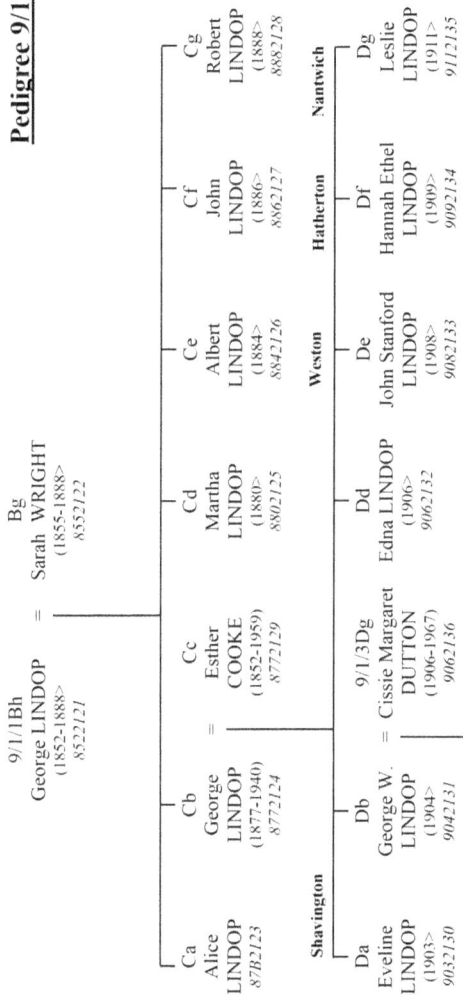

9/1/1Bh
George LINDOP
(1852-1888>
852121
=
Bg
Sarah WRIGHT
(1855-1888>
852122

**Ca**
Alice
LINDOP
87B2123

**Cb**
George
LINDOP
(1877-1940)
877124
=
**Cc**
Esther
COOKE
(1852-1959)
877129

**Cd**
Martha
LINDOP
(1880>
880125

**Ce**
Albert
LINDOP
(1884>
884126

**Weston**

**Cf**
John
LINDOP
(1886>
886127

**Hatherton**

**Cg**
Robert
LINDOP
(1888>
888128

**Nantwich**

**Da**
Eveline
LINDOP
(1903>
903130

**Db**
George W.
LINDOP
(1904>
904131

=
9/1/3Dg
Cissie Margaret
DUTTON
(1906-1967)
906136

3 children

**Dd**
Edna LINDOP
(1906>
906132

**De**
John Stanford
LINDOP
(1908>
908133

**Df**
Hannah Ethel
LINDOP
(1909>
909134

**Dg**
Leslie
LINDOP
(1911>
911135

**Shavington**

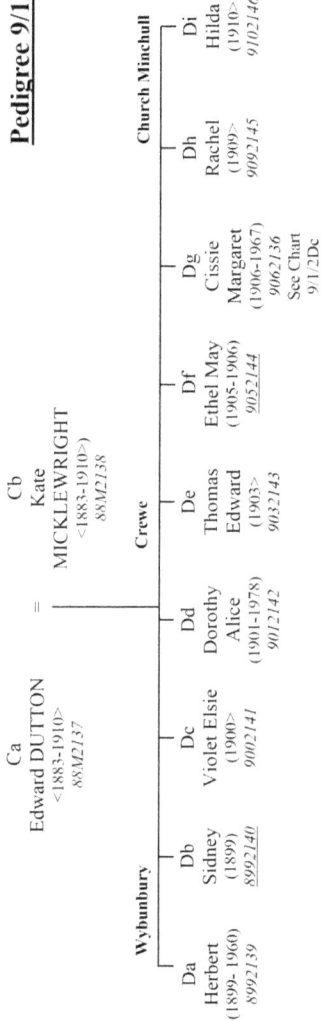

**Ca**
Edward DUTTON
<1883-1910>
88M2137
=
**Cb**
Kate
MICKLEWRIGHT
<1883-1910>
88M2138

**Crewe**

**Da**
Herbert
(1899-1960)
899139

**Db**
Sidney
(1899)
899240

**Dc**
Violet Elsie
(1900>
900241

**Dd**
Dorothy
Alice
(1901-1978)
901242

**De**
Thomas
Edward
(1903>
903243

**Df**
Ethel May
(1905-1906)
905244

**Dg**
Cissie
Margaret
(1906-1967)
906236
See Chart
9/1/2Dc

**Dh**
Rachel
(1909>
909245

**Di**
Hilda
(1910>
910246

**Wybunbury**

**Church Minshull**

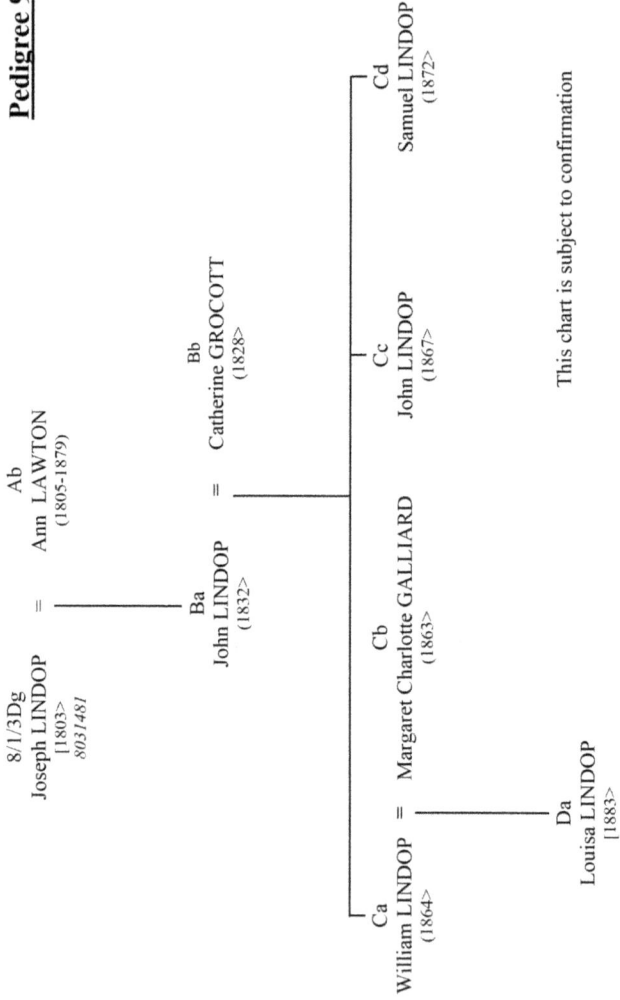

8/1/3Dg
Joseph LINDOP
[1803>
*8031481*

=

Ab
Ann LAWTON
(1805-1879)

Ba
John LINDOP
(1832>

=

Bb
Catherine GROCOTT
(1828>

Ca
William LINDOP
(1864>

=

Cb
Margaret Charlotte GALLIARD
(1863>

Cc
John LINDOP
(1867>

Cd
Samuel LINDOP
(1872>

Da
Louisa LINDOP
[1883>

This chart is subject to confirmation

**Pedigree 9/3/1**

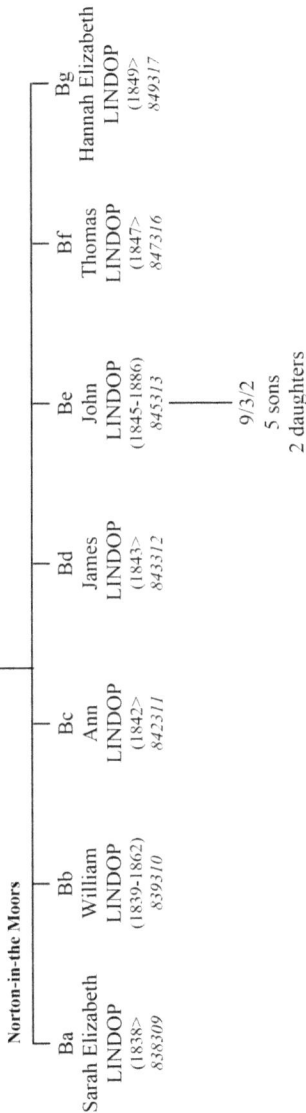

8/2/4Eb
William LINDOP
(1814-1883)
*8/4304*

=

Ab
Hannah COMPTON
(1813-1898)
*8/3305*

**Norton-in-the Moors**

Ba
Sarah Elizabeth
LINDOP
(1838>
*838309*

Bb
William
LINDOP
(1839-1862)
*839310*

Bc
Ann
LINDOP
(1842>
*842311*

Bd
James
LINDOP
(1843>
*843312*

Be
John
LINDOP
(1845-1886)
*845313*

9/3/2
5 sons
2 daughters

Bf
Thomas
LINDOP
(1847>
*847316*

Bg
Hannah Elizabeth
LINDOP
(1849>
*849317*

# Pedigree 9/3/2

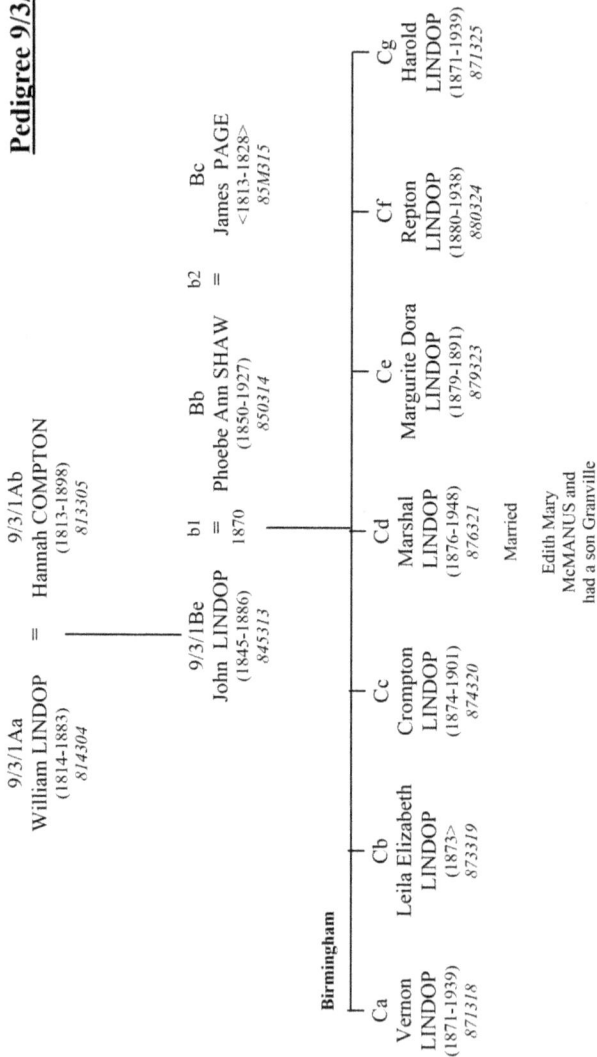

**Birmingham**

9/3/1Aa
William LINDOP
(1814-1883)
*814304*

=

9/3/1Ab
Hannah COMPTON
(1813-1898)
*813305*

Bc
James PAGE
<1813-1828>
*85M315*

9/3/1Be
John LINDOP
(1845-1886)
*845313*

b1
=
1870

Bb
Phoebe Ann SHAW
(1850-1927)
*850314*

b2
=

Ca
Vernon
LINDOP
(1871-1939)
*871318*

Cb
Leila Elizabeth
LINDOP
(1873>
*873319*

Cc
Crompton
LINDOP
(1874-1901)
*874320*

Cd
Marshal
LINDOP
(1876-1948)
*876321*

Ce
Margurite Dora
LINDOP
(1879-1891)
*879323*

Cf
Repton
LINDOP
(1880-1938)
*880324*

Cg
Harold
LINDOP
(1871-1939)
*871325*

Married

Edith Mary
McMANUS and
had a son Granville

**Chipnal, near Cheswardine**

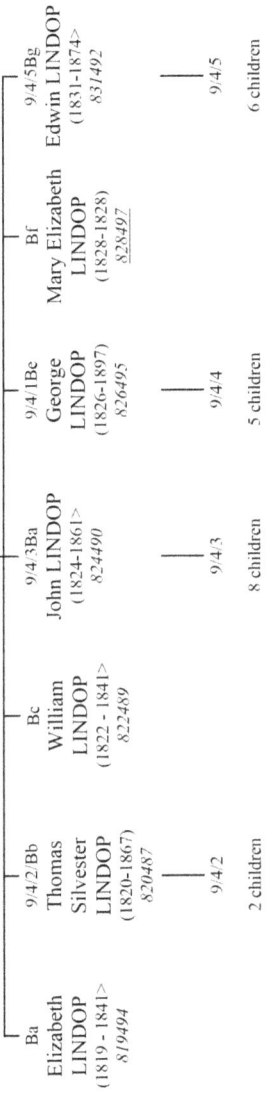

8/2/9Da
William LINDOP = Mary SILVESTER
(1785-1848)        (1783-1878)
785139             783168

8/2/9Db

Ba
Elizabeth
LINDOP
(1819 - 1841>
819494

9/4/2Bb
Thomas
Silvester
LINDOP
(1820-1867)
820487

Bc
William
LINDOP
(1822 - 1841>
822489

9/4/3Ba
John LINDOP
(1824-1861>
824490

9/4/1Be
George
LINDOP
(1826-1897)
826495

Bf
Mary Elizabeth
LINDOP
(1828-1828)
828497

9/4/5Bg
Edwin LINDOP
(1831-1874>
831492

9/4/2

2 children

9/4/3

8 children

9/4/4

5 children

9/4/5

6 children

# Pedigree 9/4/2

| | |
|---|---|
| Ae | Penelope (1802-1876) 8021658 |
| Bh | Annie HOLLAND |

Ad George POWELL <1825-1841> 82M1657 = Bg Henry GREGORY

Ac John WILLETT <1820-1837> 81M1145

**Chipnal**

8/2/9Da William LINDOP (1785-1848) 785139 = 8/2/9Db Mary SILVESTER (1783-1878) 783168

**Acton**

Bc Elizabeth WILLETT (1837-1871> 837488

Bd George Henry POWELL (1841-1871> 8411077

**Woore**

Bf Emma Henry (1839> (1843>

Ch Annie Maria GREGORY (1877-1909> **Morton Say** 8771656

Cg Richard Willet POWELL (1870-1909> 8701147 = 

Cf Alfred F POWELL (1874>

Ce Joseph POWELL (1875>

Cd Emma POWELL (1878>

c2 = 

Dc Edgar Richard POWELL (1909-1934> 9091661 = Dd Ethel Mary MATTHEWS (1911-1934> 9111662

**Sandyford**

9/4/1Bb Thomas Silvester LINDOP (1820-1867) 820487 = c1

Cc William LINDOP (1867> 867569

Cb Elizabeth LINDOP (1866-1889) 866568

Ba James LAWTON (1830-1908) 830564

Ca Frank William LAWTON (1854-1951) **Audlem** 854567 = 

Da Frederick William LAWTON (1889-1964) **Stoke-on-Trent** 889570

Db Christina WALTER (1891-1976) **Stoke-on-Trent** 891571

Ea Edid LAWTON

Eb James Lindop LAWTON

**Note:** Cd, Ce, Cf and Cg are shown in reverse chronological order for simplicity.

**Chipnal**  **Hinstock**  **Woore**  **Tyreley**  **Blore**

8/2/9Da
William LINDOP = Mary SILVESTER
(1785-1848)    (1783-1878)
785139         783168

Ac
John LEA
(1789-1879)
7892046

=

8/2/15Dc
Jane SILVESTER
(1798-1889)
7982045

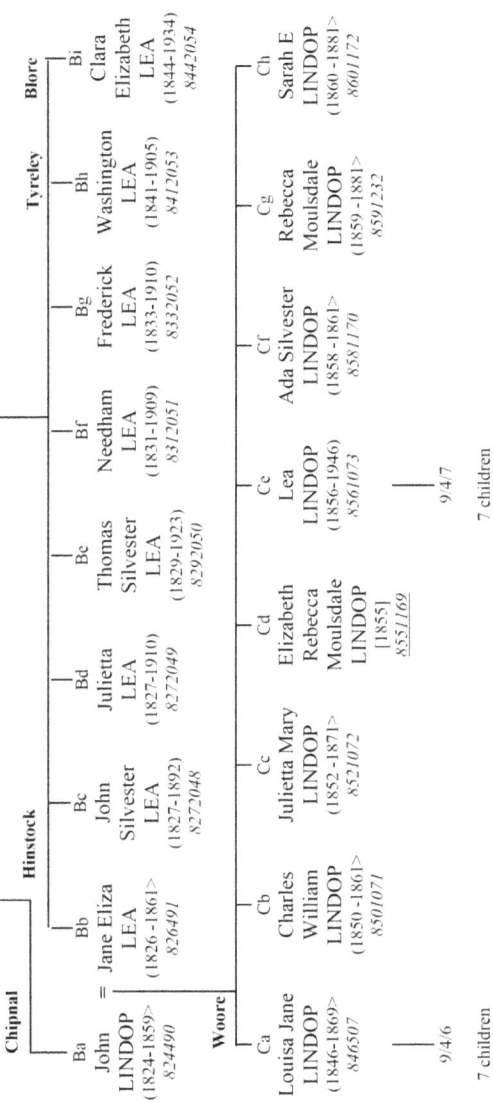

Ba
John
LINDOP
(1824-1859>
824490

=

Bb
Jane Eliza
LEA
(1826-1861>
826491

Bc
John
Silvester
LEA
(1827-1892)
8272048

Bd
Julietta
LEA
(1827-1910)
8272049

Bc
Thomas
Silvester
LEA
(1829-1923)
8292050

Bf
Needham
LEA
(1831-1909)
8312051

Bg
Frederick
LEA
(1833-1910)
8332052

Bh
Washington
LEA
(1841-1905)
8412053

Bi
Clara
Elizabeth
LEA
(1844-1934)
8442054

Ca
Louisa Jane
LINDOP
(1846-1869>
846507

Cb
Charles
William
LINDOP
(1850-1861>
8501071

Cc
Julietta Mary
LINDOP
(1852-1871>
8521072

Cd
Elizabeth
Rebecca
Moulsdale
LINDOP
[1855]
8551169

Ce
Lea
LINDOP
(1856-1946)
8561073

Cf
Ada Silvester
LINDOP
(1858-1861>
8581170

Cg
Rebecca
Moulsdale
LINDOP
(1859-1881>
8591232

Ch
Sarah E
LINDOP
(1860-1881>
8601172

9/4/6

7 children

9/4/7

7 children

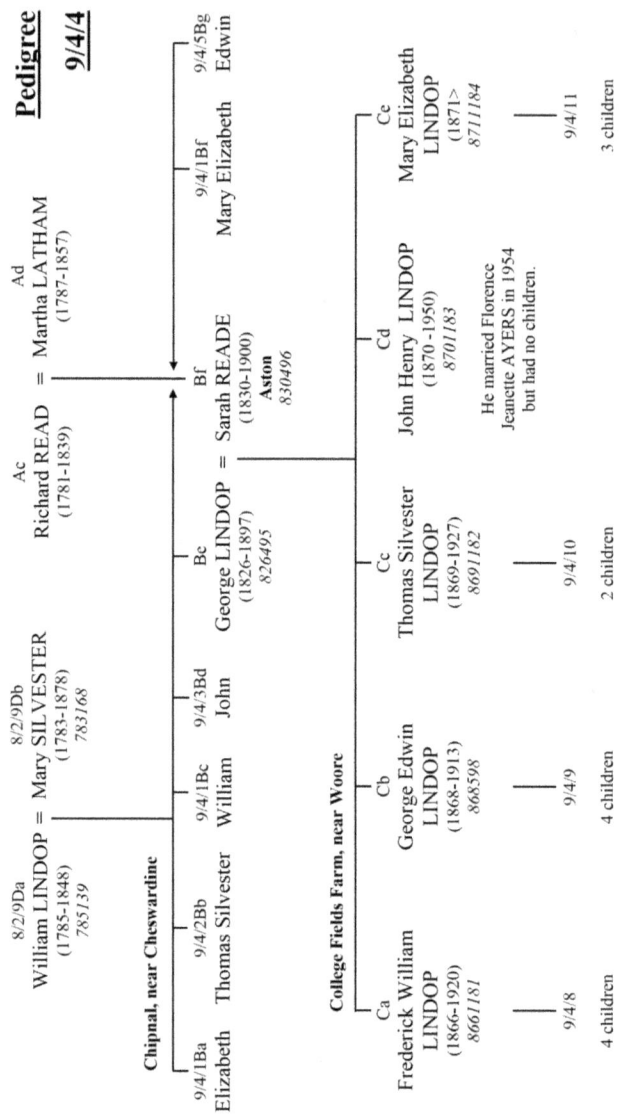

Ac
Richard READE = Martha LATHAM
(1781-1839)        (1787-1857)
                        Ad

8/2/9Da
William LINDOP = Mary SILVESTER
(1785-1848)        (1783-1878)
785139                783168
                        8/2/9Db

**Chipnal, near Cheswardine**

9/4/1Ba        9/4/2Bb        9/4/1Bc        9/4/3Bd
Elizabeth      Thomas Silvester   William         John

Bc
George LINDOP = Sarah READE
(1826-1897)        (1830-1900)
826495                **Aston**
                         830496
                         Bf

9/4/1Bf        9/4/5Bg
Mary Elizabeth   Edwin

**College Fields Farm, near Woore**

Ca
Frederick William
LINDOP
(1866-1920)
866181

9/4/8

4 children

Cb
George Edwin
LINDOP
(1868-1913)
868598

9/4/9

4 children

Cc
Thomas Silvester
LINDOP
(1869-1927)
869182

9/4/10

2 children

Cd
John Henry LINDOP
(1870-1950)
870183

He married Florence
Jeanette AYERS in 1954
but had no children.

Ce
Mary Elizabeth
LINDOP
(1871>)
871184

9/4/11

3 children

# Pedigree 9/4/5

Ac
Isaac GILBERT
*81M1173*

Ad
Elizabeth
*81M1174*

8/2/9Da
William LINDOP = Mary SILVESTER
(1785-1848)        (1783-1878)
*785139*              *783/68*

**Chipnal, near Cheswardine**

Bh
Mary Ann
GILBERT
<1835-1871>
**High Offley**
*82B493*

Bg
Edwin
LINDOP
(1831-1901>
*831492*

=

9/4/1Ba
Elizabeth

9/4/2Bb
Thomas Silvester

9/4/1Bc
William

9/4/3Bd
John

9/4/4Bc
George

9/4/1Bf
Mary Elizabeth

**Mucklestone**

Ca
William Edwin
Gilbert LINDOP
(1853>
*853588*

Cb
George Thomas
LINDOP
(1857>
*857586*

Cc
Henry Isaac
LINDOP
(1859>
*859587*

Cd
Clare Annie
LINDOP
(1864>
*864589*

Ce
Mary E. LINDOP
(1865>
*865590*

Cf
John LINDOP
(1871>
*87/591*

# Pedigree

## 9/4/6

8/2/9Da
William LINDOP = Mary SILVESTER 8/2/9Db
(1785-1848)      (1783-1878)
785139            783168

9/4/3Ac
John LEA
(1789-1879)
7892046
=
Jane SILVESTER 8/2/15Dc
(1798-1889)
7982045

**Chipnal**

Ba
John
LINDOP
(1824-1859>
824490

Bb
= Jane Eliza
LEA
(1826-1861>
826491

**Hinstock**

| 9/4/3Bc | 9/4/3Bd | 9/4/3Be | 9/4/3Bf | 9/4/3Bg | 9/4/3Bh | 9/4/3Bi |
|---|---|---|---|---|---|---|
| John Silvester LEA | Julietta LEA | Thomas Silvester LEA | Needham LEA | Frederick LEA | Washington LEA | Clara Elizabeth LEA |
| (1827-1892) | (1827-1910) | (1829-1923) | (1831-1909) | (1833-1910) | (1841-1905) | (1844-1934) |
| 8272048 | 8272049 | 8292050 | 8312051 | 8332052 | 8412053 | 8442054 |

**Tyreley**   **Blore**

**Woore**

Ca
Louisa Jane
LINDOP
(1846-1869>
846507

Cb
= William
SYMCOX
84M506

| 9/4/3Cb | 9/4/3Cc | 9/4/3Cd | 9/4/3Ce | 9/4/3Cf | 9/4/3Cg | 9/4/3Ch |
|---|---|---|---|---|---|---|
| Charles William LINDOP | Julietta Mary LINDOP | Elizabeth Rebecca Moulsdale LINDOP | Lea LINDOP | Ada Silvester LINDOP | Rebecca Moulsdale LINDOP | Sarah E LINDOP |
| (1850-1861> | (1852-1871> | [1855] | (1856-1946) | (1858-1861> | (1859-1881> | (1860-1881> |
| 8501071 | 8521072 | _8551169_ | 8561073 | 8581170 | 8591232 | 8601172 |

**Ashley**

| Da | Cb | Cc | Cd | Ce | Cf | Cg |
|---|---|---|---|---|---|---|
| Louisa Mary SYMCOX | Margaret SYMCOX | Eunice Annie SYMCOX | Lizzie Emma SYMCOX | William SYMCOX | John SYMCOX | Claude SYMCOX |
| (1869-1910> | 88E1194 | 88E1192 | 88E1196 | 88E1197 | 88E1199 | 88M1201 |
| 869509 | | | | | | |
| Married Enoch BARTRAM | Married William THORNLEY | Married Hugo DEAVILLE | Married John SALT | Married Henrietta MEESON | Married Agatha MACNISH | Married Kathleen |
| Children: William Sturgess, Winifred Mary | Children: Arthur, William, Ida | | Child: Melville John | Child: William | Child: John Leonard | |

8/2/9Da
William LINDOP = Mary SILVESTER
(1785-1848)         (1783-1878)
785139                783168

8/2/9Db

9/4/3Ac
John LEA
(1789-1879)
7892046

=

8/2/15Dc
Jane SILVESTER
(1798-1889)
7982045

9/4/3Ba
John
LINDOP
(1824-1850>
824490

=

9/4/3Bb
Jane Eliza
LEA
(1826>
8262047

9/4/3Bc
John
Silvester
LEA
(1827-1892)
8272048

9/4/3Bd
Julietta
LEA
(1827-1910)
8272049

9/4/3Bc
Thomas
Silvester
LEA
(1829-1923)

9/4/3Bf
Needham
LEA
(1831-1909)
8312051

9/4/3Bg
Frederick
LEA
(1833-1910)
8332052

9/4/3Bh
Washington
LEA
(1841-1905)
8412053

9/4/3Bi
Clara
Elizabeth
LEA
(1844-1934)
8442054

9/4/3Ca
Louisa

9/4/3Cb
Charles

9/4/3Cc
Julietta

9/4/3Cd
Elizabeth

Ce
Lea LINDOP
(1856-1946)
8561073

=

Cf
Harriet BEARDSMORE
(1847-1908>
8471217

9/4/3Cf
Ada

9/4/3Cg
Rebecca

9/4/3Ch
Sarah

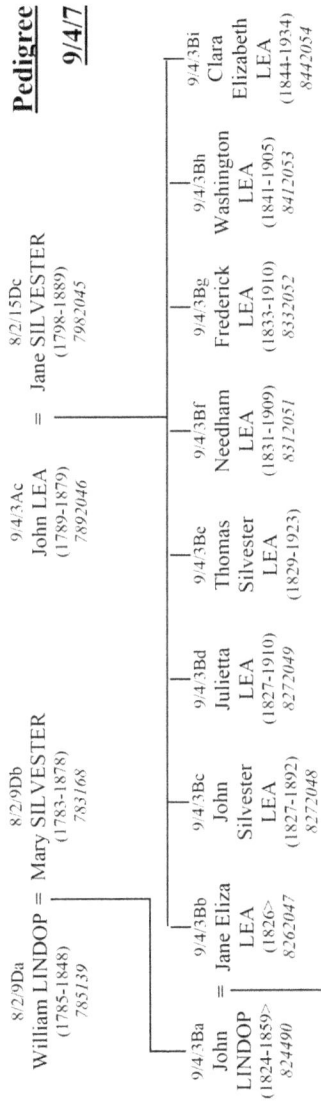

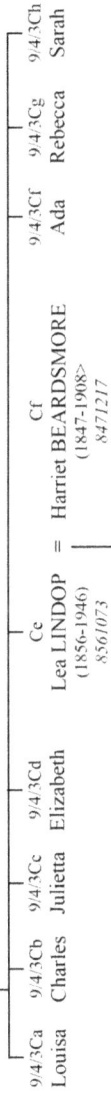

**Newcastle under Lyme**

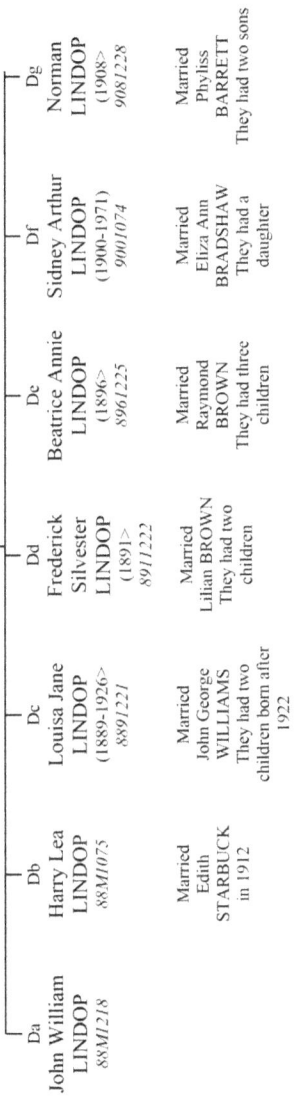

Da
John William
LINDOP
88MI218

Db
Harry Lea
LINDOP
88MI1075

Married
Edith
STARBUCK
in 1912

Dc
Louisa Jane
LINDOP
(1889-1926>
8891221

Married
John George
WILLIAMS
They had two
children born after
1922

Dd
Frederick
Silvester
LINDOP
(1891>
8911222

Married
Lilian BROWN.
They had two
children

Dc
Beatrice Annie
LINDOP
(1896>
8961225

Married
Raymond
BROWN
They had three
children

Df
Sidney Arthur
LINDOP
(1900-1971)
9001074

Married
Eliza Ann
BRADSHAW
They had a
daughter

Dg
Norman
LINDOP
(1908>
9081228

Married
Phyliss
BARRETT
They had two sons

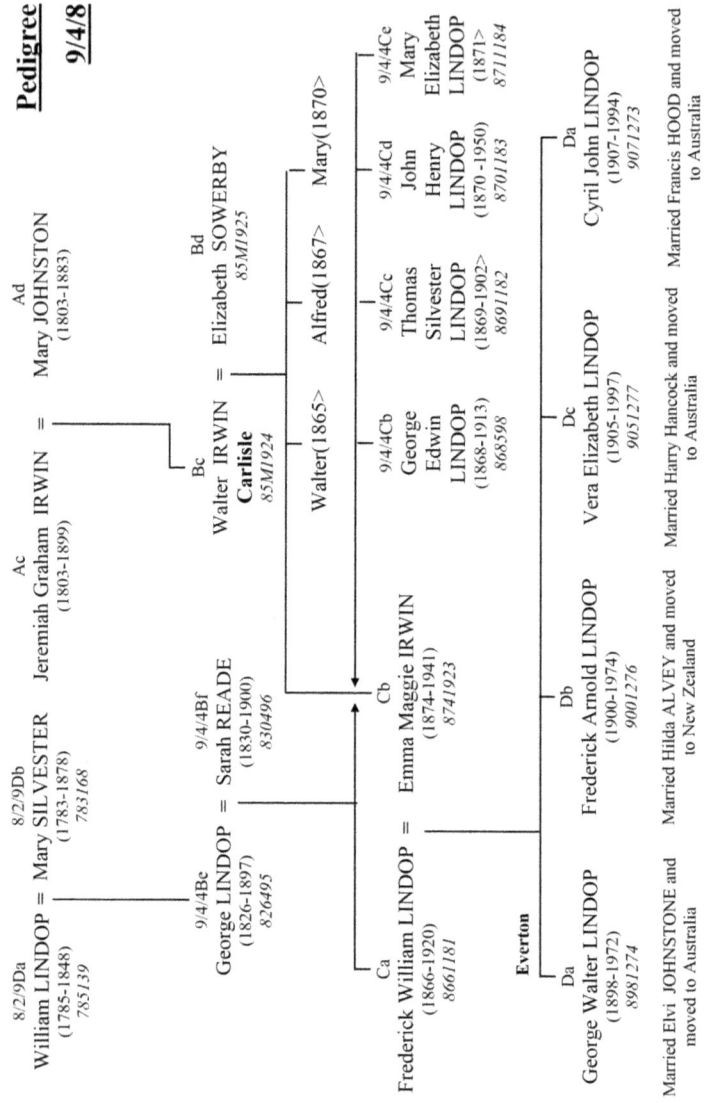

**Ad**
Mary JOHNSTON
(1803-1883)

**Ac**
Jeremiah Graham  IRWIN
(1803-1899)
=

8/2/9Db
Mary SILVESTER
(1783-1878)
*783168*

8/2/9Da
William LINDOP
(1785-1848)
*785139*
=

**Bd**
Elizabeth  SOWERBY
*85M1925*

**Bc**
Walter  IRWIN
**Carlisle**
*85M1924*
=

9/4/4Bf
Sarah READE
(1830-1900)
*830496*

9/4/4Be
George LINDOP
(1826-1897)
*826495*
=

Walter(1865>       Alfred(1867>       Mary(1870>

9/4/4Ce
Mary
Elizabeth
LINDOP
(1871>
*8711184*

9/4/4Cd
John
Henry
LINDOP
(1870 -1950)
*8701183*

9/4/4Cc
Thomas
Silvester
LINDOP
(1869-1902>
*8691182*

9/4/4Cb
George
Edwin
LINDOP
(1868-1913)
*868598*

**Cb**
Emma Maggie IRWIN
(1874-1941)
*8741923*

**Ca**
Frederick William LINDOP
(1866-1920)
*8661181*
=

**Everton**

**Da**
Cyril John LINDOP
(1907-1994)
*9071273*
Married Francis HOOD and moved
to Australia

**Dc**
Vera Elizabeth LINDOP
(1905-1997)
*9051277*
Married Harry Hancock and moved
to Australia

**Db**
Frederick Arnold LINDOP
(1900-1974)
*9001276*
Married Hilda ALVEY and moved
to New Zealand

**Da**
George Walter LINDOP
(1898-1972)
*8981274*
Married Elvi JOHNSTONE and
moved to Australia

# Pedigree 9/4/9

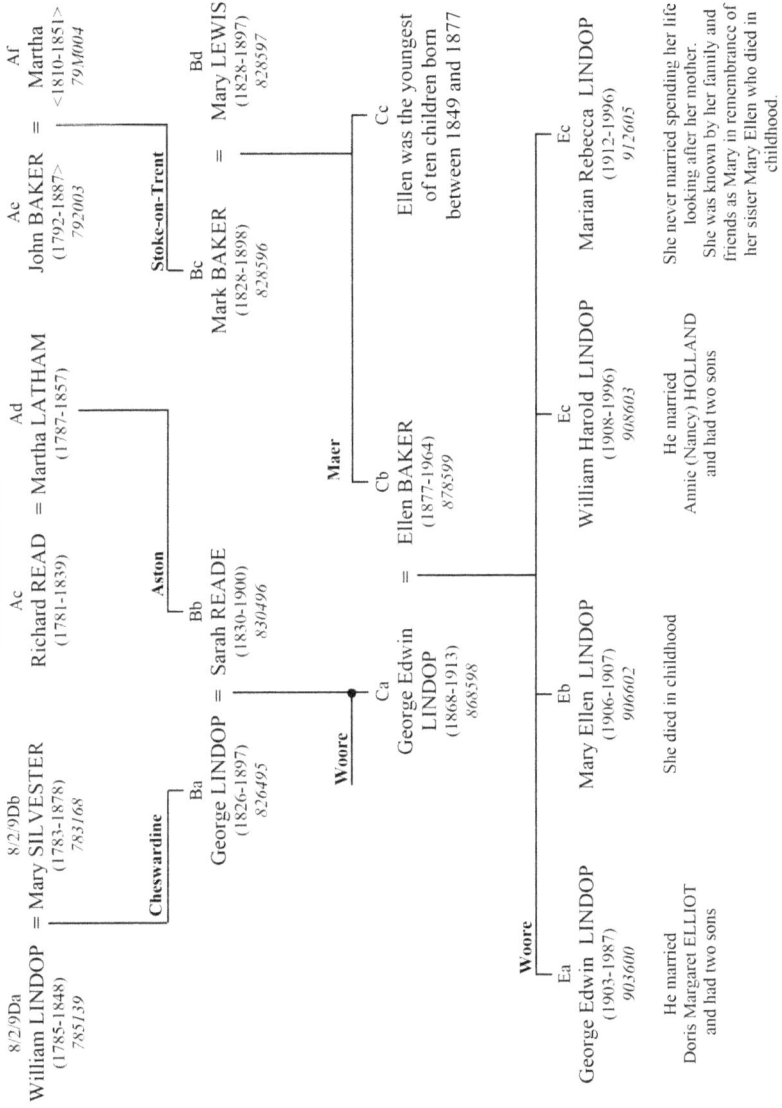

**Cheswardine**

8/2/9Da
William LINDOP
(1785-1848)
*785139*

8/2/9Db
= Mary SILVESTER
(1783-1878)
*783168*

Ac
Richard READ = Martha LATHAM
(1781-1839)        (1787-1857)

Ae
John BAKER =
(1792-1887)
<792003>

Af
Martha
<1810-1851>
*793M004*

**Stoke-on-Trent**

Ba
George LINDOP = Sarah READE
(1826-1897)        (1830-1900)
*826495*            *830496*

**Aston**

Bb

Bc
Mark BAKER =
(1828-1898)
*828596*

Bd
Mary LEWIS
(1828-1897)
*828597*

**Woore**

Ca
George Edwin
LINDOP
(1868-1913)
*868598*

=

**Maer**

Cb
Ellen BAKER
(1877-1964)
*878599*

Cc
Ellen was the youngest
of ten children born
between 1849 and 1877

**Woore**

Ea
George Edwin LINDOP
(1903-1987)
*903600*

He married
Doris Margaret ELLIOT
and had two sons

Eb
Mary Ellen LINDOP
(1906-1907)
*906602*

She died in childhood

Ec
William Harold LINDOP
(1908-1996)
*908603*

He married
Annie (Nancy) HOLLAND
and had two sons

Ec
Marian Rebecca LINDOP
(1912-1996)
*912605*

She never married spending her life
looking after her mother.
She was known by her family and
friends as Mary in remembrance of
her sister Mary Ellen who died in
childhood.

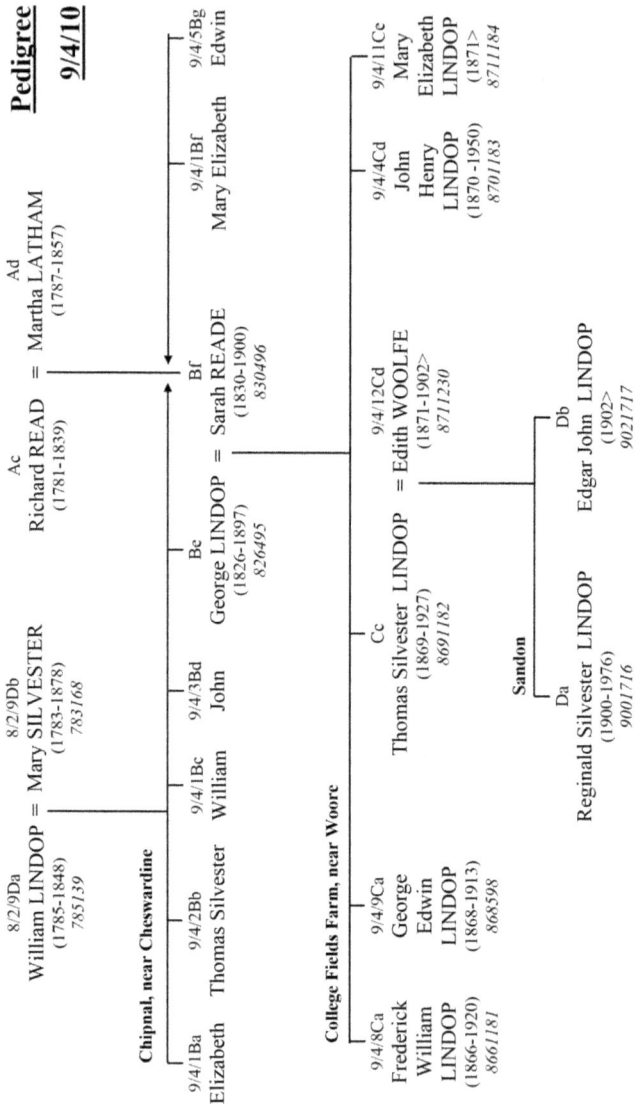

Ac
Richard READ
(1781-1839)

Ad
Martha LATHAM
(1787-1857)

=

8/2/9Da
William LINDOP
(1785-1848)
785139

=

8/2/9Db
Mary SILVESTER
(1783-1878)
783168

**Chipnal, near Cheswardine**

9/4/1Ba
Elizabeth

9/4/2Bb
Thomas Silvester

9/4/1Bc
William

9/4/3Bd
John

Be
George LINDOP
(1826-1897)
826495

=

Bf
Sarah READE
(1830-1900)
830496

9/4/1Bf
Mary Elizabeth

9/4/5Bg
Edwin

**College Fields Farm, near Woore**

9/4/8Ca
Frederick
William
LINDOP
(1866-1920)
8661181

9/4/9Ca
George
Edwin
LINDOP
(1868-1913)
868598

Cc
Thomas Silvester LINDOP
(1869-1927)
8691182

=

9/412Cd
Edith WOOLFE
(1871-1902>
8711230

9/4/4Cd
John
Henry
LINDOP
(1870 -1950)
8701183

9/4/11Ce
Mary
Elizabeth
LINDOP
(1871>
8711184

**Sandon**

Da
Reginald Silvester LINDOP
(1900-1976)
9001716

Db
Edgar John LINDOP
(1902>
9021717

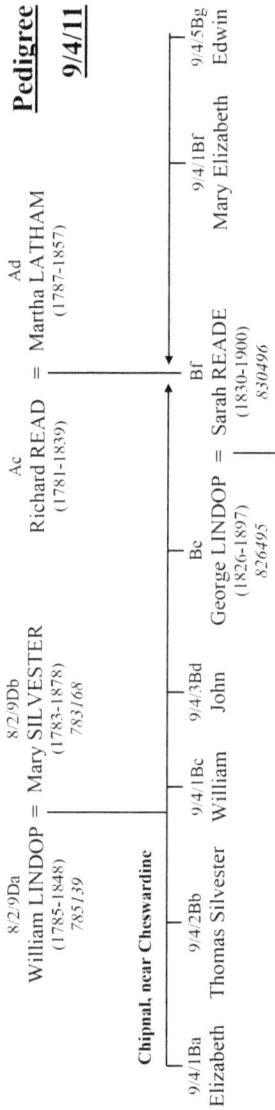

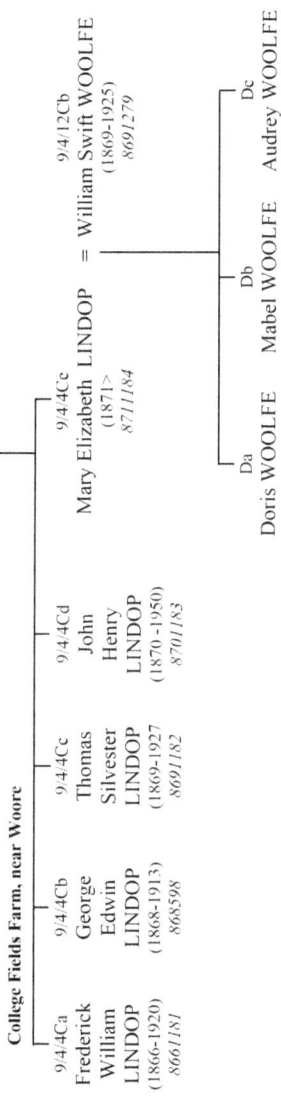

Ac
Richard READ
(1781-1839)

Ad
Martha LATHAM
(1787-1857)

=

8/2/9Da
William LINDOP
(1785-1848)
*785139*

=

8/2/9Db
Mary SILVESTER
(1783-1878)
*783168*

**Chipnal, near Cheswardine**

9/4/1Ba
Elizabeth

9/4/2Bb
Thomas Silvester

9/4/1Bc
William

9/4/3Bd
John

Be
George LINDOP
(1826-1897)
*826495*

=

Bf
Sarah READE
(1830-1900)
*830496*

9/4/1Bf
Mary Elizabeth

9/4/5Bg
Edwin

**College Fields Farm, near Woore**

9/4/4Ca
Frederick
William
LINDOP
(1866-1920)
*866118I*

9/4/4Cb
George
Edwin
LINDOP
(1868-1913)
*868598*

9/4/4Cc
Thomas
Silvester
LINDOP
(1869-1927)
*869I182*

9/4/4Cd
John
Henry
LINDOP
(1870-1950)
*870I183*

9/4/4Ce
Mary Elizabeth LINDOP
(1871>
*871I184*

=

9/4/12Cb
William Swift WOOLFE
(1869-1925)
*869I279*

Da
Doris WOOLFE

Db
Mabel WOOLFE

Dc
Audrey WOOLFE

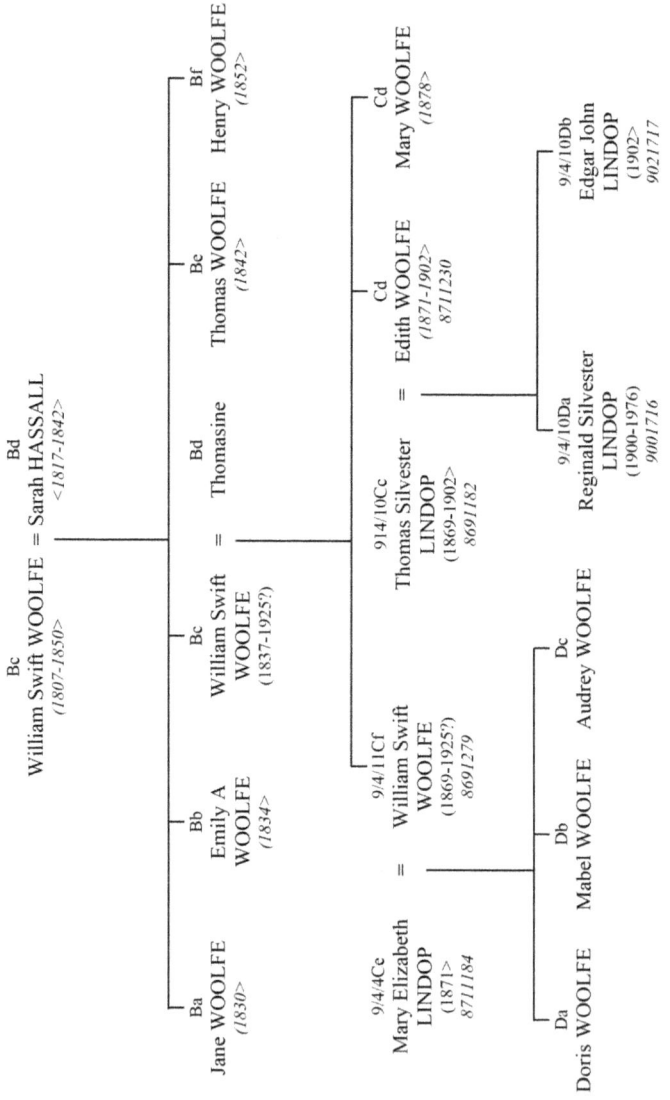

Bc
William Swift WOOLFE = Sarah HASSALL
*(1807-1850>*  Bd  *<1817-1842>*

Ba
Jane WOOLFE
*(1830>*

Bb
Emily A
WOOLFE
*(1834>*

Bc
William Swift
WOOLFE
*(1837-1925?)*

Bd
Thomasine

Be
Thomas WOOLFE
*(1842>*

Bf
Henry WOOLFE
*(1852>*

9/4/4Ce
Mary Elizabeth
LINDOP
*(1871>*
*8711184*

=

9/4/11Cf
William Swift
WOOLFE
*(1869-1925?)*
*8691279*

914/10Cc
Thomas Silvester
LINDOP
*(1869-1902>*
*8691182*

=

Cd
Edith WOOLFE
*(1871-1902>*
*8711230*

Cd
Mary WOOLFE
*(1878>*

Da
Doris WOOLFE

Db
Mabel WOOLFE

Dc
Audrey WOOLFE

9/4/10Da
Reginald Silvester
LINDOP
*(1900-1976)*
*9001716*

9/4/10Db
Edgar John
LINDOP
*(1902>*
*9021717*

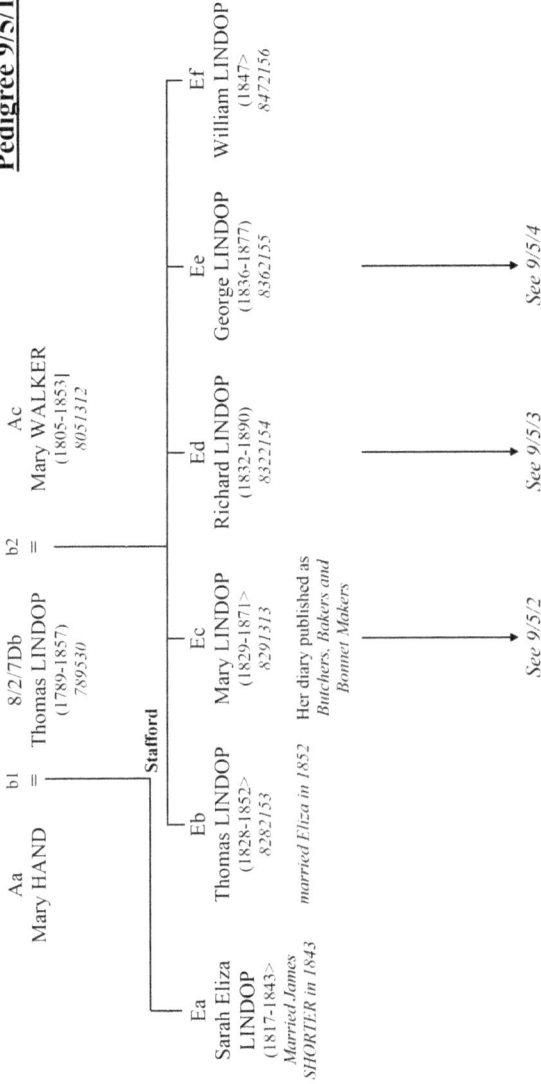

**Pedigree 9/5/1**

Aa
Mary HAND

b1
=

8/2/7Db
Thomas LINDOP
(1789-1857)
789530

b2
=

Ac
Mary WALKER
(1805-1853]
8051312

**Stafford**

Ea
Sarah Eliza
LINDOP
(1817-1843>
Married James
SHORTER in 1843

Eb
Thomas LINDOP
(1828-1852>
8282153

Ec
Mary LINDOP
(1829-1871>
8291313

Ed
Richard LINDOP
(1832-1890)
8322154

Ee
George LINDOP
(1836-1877)
8362155

Ef
William LINDOP
(1847>
8472156

*married Eliza in 1852*

*Her diary published as
Butchers, Bakers and
Bonnet Makers*

*See 9/5/2*

*See 9/5/3*

*See 9/5/4*

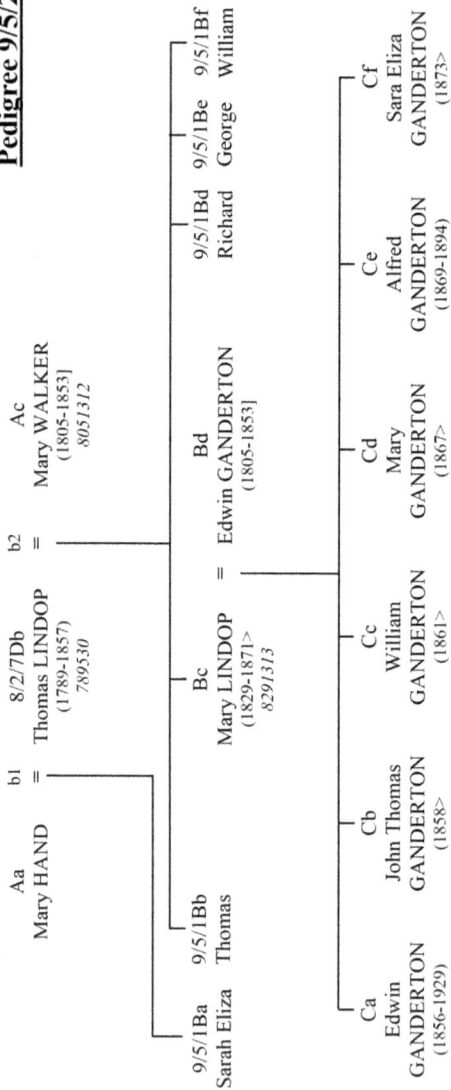

Aa
Mary HAND

b1
=

8/2/7Db
Thomas LINDOP
(1789-1857)
*789530*

b2
=

Ac
Mary WALKER
[1805-1853]
*8051312*

9/5/1Bb
Thomas

Bc
Mary LINDOP
(1829-1871>
*8291313*

=

Bd
Edwin GANDERTON
[1805-1853]

9/5/1Bd    9/5/1Be    9/5/1Bf
Richard    George     William

9/5/1Ba
Sarah Eliza

Ca
Edwin
GANDERTON
(1856-1929)

Cb
John Thomas
GANDERTON
(1858>

Cc
William
GANDERTON
(1861>

Cd
Mary
GANDERTON
(1867>

Ce
Alfred
GANDERTON
(1869-1894)

Cf
Sara Eliza
GANDERTON
(1873>

## Pedigree 9/5/3

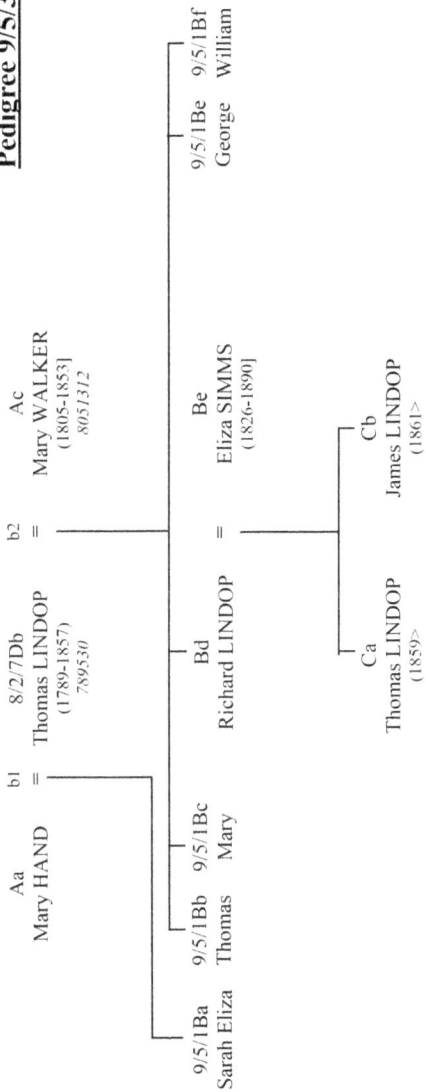

Aa      b1
Mary HAND    =

8/2/7Db
Thomas LINDOP
(1789-1857)
*789530*

b2      Ac
=      Mary WALKER
[1805-1853]
*8051312*

9/5/1Ba    9/5/1Bb    9/5/1Bc
Sarah Eliza    Thomas    Mary

Bd
Richard LINDOP    =

Be
Eliza SIMMS
[1826-1890]

9/5/1Be    9/5/1Bf
George    William

Ca
Thomas LINDOP
(1859>

Cb
James LINDOP
(1861>

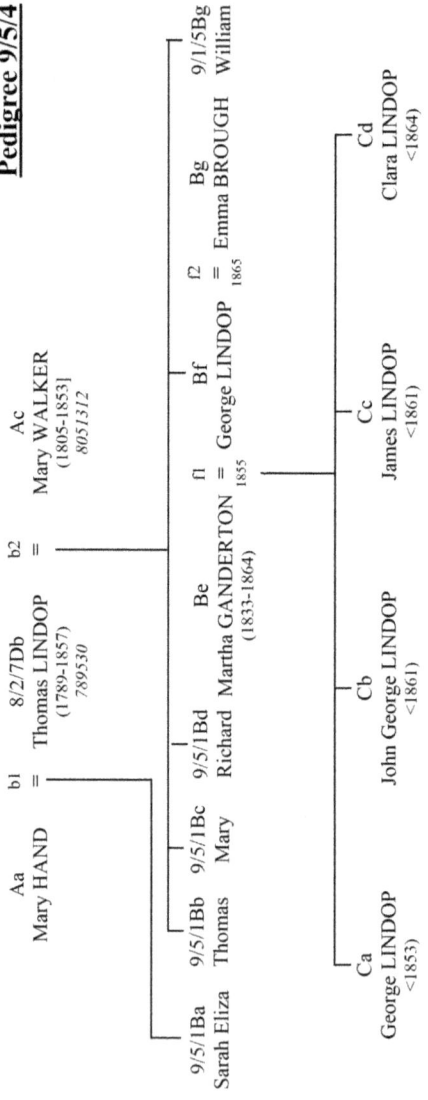

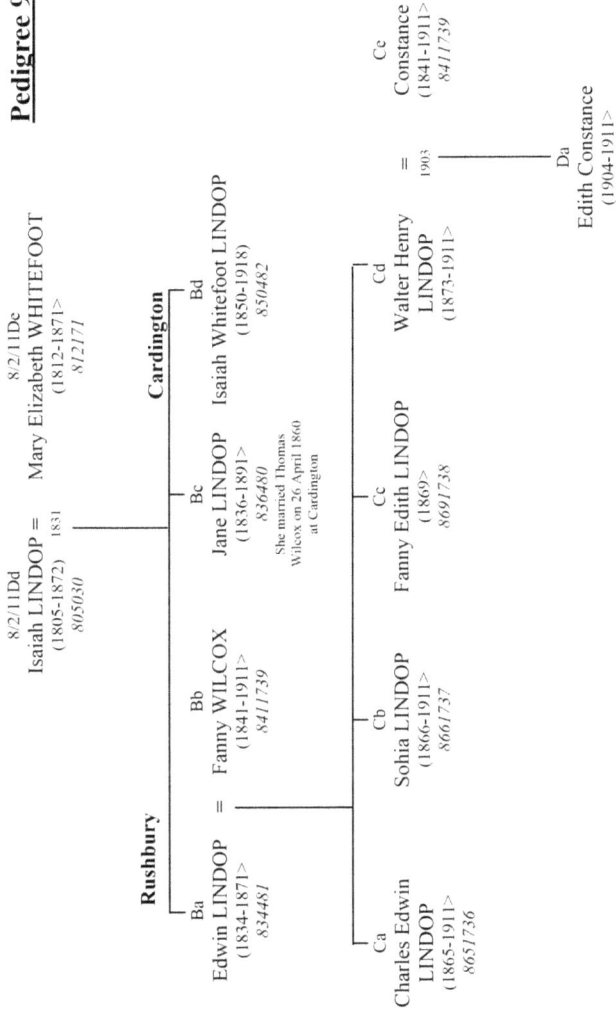

**Rushbury**

**Cardington**

8/2/11Dd
Isaiah LINDOP = 1831
(1805-1872)
*805030*

8/2/11De
Mary Elizabeth WHITEFOOT
(1812-1871>
*812171*

Ba
Edwin LINDOP
(1834-1871>
*834481*

= Bb
Fanny WILCOX
(1841-1911>
*8411739*

Bc
Jane LINDOP
(1836-1891>
*836480*

She married Thomas
Wilcox on 26 April 1860
at Cardington

Bd
Isaiah Whitefoot LINDOP
(1850-1918)
*850482*

Ca
Charles Edwin
LINDOP
(1865-1911>
*8651736*

Cb
Sohia LINDOP
(1866-1911>
*8661737*

Cc
Fanny Edith LINDOP
(1869>
*8691738*

Cd
Walter Henry
LINDOP
(1873-1911>

Ce
Constance
(1841-1911>
*8411739*

Da
Edith Constance
(1904-1911>

= 1903

**Rushbury**

**Cardington**

8/2/11Dd
Isaiah LINDOP = 1831
(1805-1872)
*805030*

8/2/11De
Mary Elizabeth WHITEFOOT
(1812-1871>
*812171*

Ba
Edwin LINDOP
(1834-1871>
*834481*

Bc
Jane LINDOP
(1836-1891>
*836480*
She married Thomas
Wilcox on 26 April 1860
at Cardington

Bd
Isaiah Whitefoot LINDOP
(1850-1918)
*850482*

Ce
Constance
(1841-1911>
*8411739*

Ca
Charles Edwin
LINDOP
(1865-1911>
*8651736*

Cb
Sohia LINDOP
(1866-1911>
*8661737*

Cc
Fanny Edith LINDOP
(1869>
*8691738*

Cd
Walter Henry
LINDOP
(1873-1911>
*873-1911>*

=
1903

Da
Edith Constance
(1904-1911>

Bb
Thomas
WILCOX
(1841-1911>
*8411739*

=

Need to research the Wilcox family

# Pedigree 9/6/3

**Rushbury**

**Cardington**

8/2/11Dd
Isaiah LINDOP = 1831
(1805-1872)
*805030*

8/2/11De
Mary Elizabeth WHITEFOOT
(1812-1871)
*812171*

Ba
Edwin LINDOP
(1834-1871>
*834481*

Bc
Jane LINDOP
(1836-1891>
*836480*
She married Thomas
Wilcox on 26 April 1860
at Cardington

Bd
Isaiah Whitefoot LINDOP
(1850-1918)
*850482*

Bb
Thomas
WILCOX
(1841-1911>
*841739*

=

Ca
Charles Edwin
LINDOP
(1865-1911>
*865736*

Cb
Sohia LINDOP
(1866-1911>
*866737*

Cc
Fanny Edith LINDOP
(1869>
*869738*

Cd
Walter Henry
LINDOP
(1873-1911>

=
1903

Ce
Constance
(1841-1911>
*841739*

Da
Edith Constance
(1904-1911>

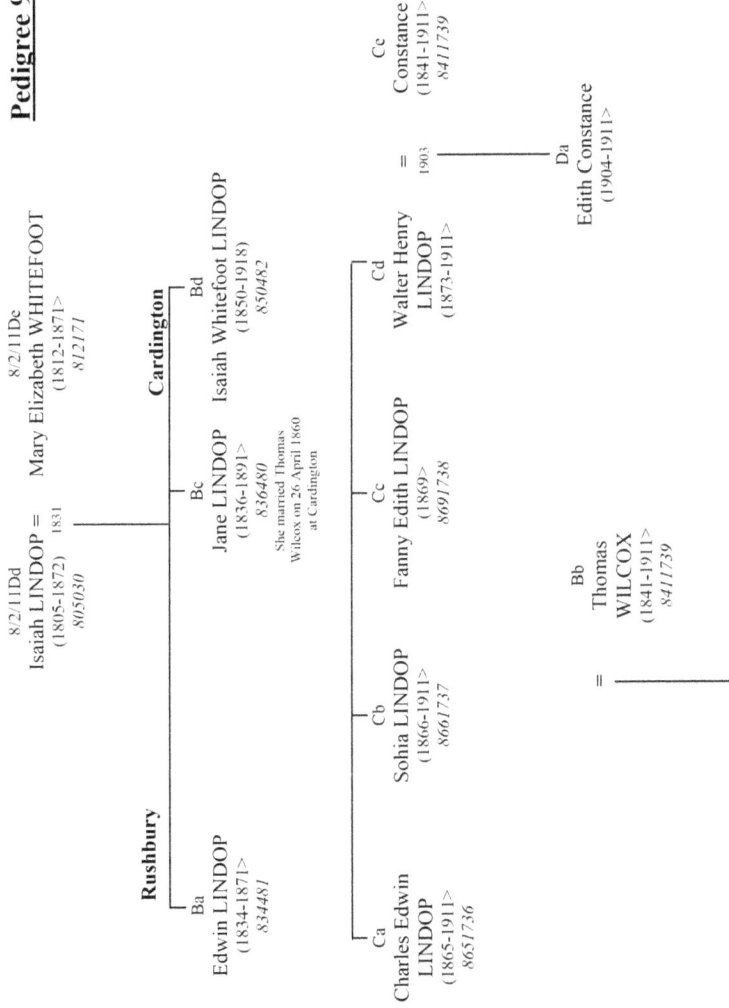

Need to research the Wilcox family

## Pedigree 9/7/1

```
        8/5/2Ea                    Ab
   Samuel LINDOP    =    Maria MITCHELL
    (1810-1885)    1831    (1807-1887)
      810372                  807373
```

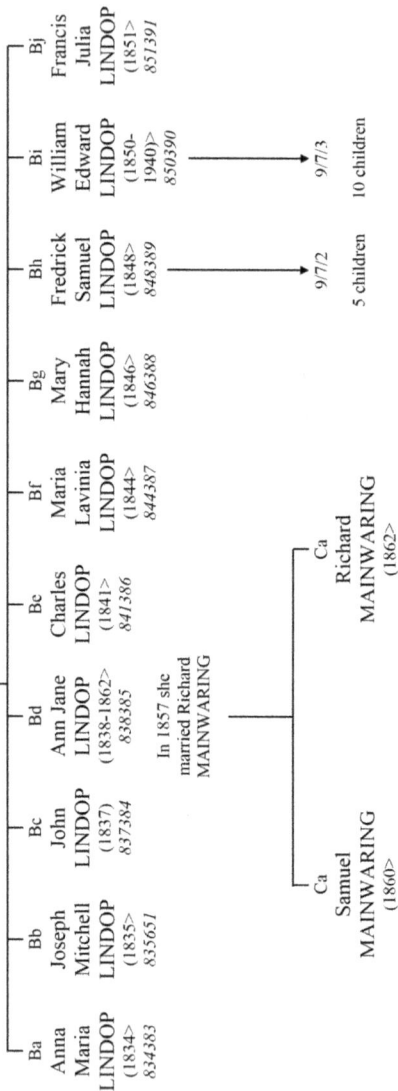

| Ba | Bb | Bc | Bd | Bc | Bf | Bg | Bh | Bi | Bj |
|---|---|---|---|---|---|---|---|---|---|
| Anna Maria LINDOP | Joseph Mitchell LINDOP | John LINDOP | Ann Jane LINDOP | Charles LINDOP | Maria Lavinia LINDOP | Mary Hannah LINDOP | Fredrick Samuel LINDOP | William Edward LINDOP | Francis Julia LINDOP |
| (1834> | (1835> | (1837) | (1838-1862> | (1841> | (1844> | (1846>388 | (1848< | (1850- | (1851> |
| 834383 | 835651 | 837384 | 838385 | 841386 | 844387 | 846388 | 848389 | 1940)> | 851391 |
|  |  |  |  |  |  |  |  | 850390 |  |

Ann Jane LINDOP:
In 1857 she married Richard MAINWARING

```
        Ca                              Ca
     Samuel                         Richard
   MAINWARING                     MAINWARING
     (1860>                          (1862>
```

Fredrick Samuel LINDOP → 9/7/2 — 5 children

William Edward LINDOP → 9/7/3 — 10 children

This chart is discussed in more detail in *Lindop: A Family History* by John Barford Lindop published by Mercianotes. (ISBN: 9781522882947 )

85/2Ea
Samuel LINDOP = Maria MITCHELL
(1810-1885)        1831        (1807-1887)
810372                              807373

| 9/7/1Ba | 9/7/1Bb | 9/7/1Bc | 9/7/1Bd | 9/7/1Be | 9/7/1Bf | 9/7/1Bg | Bh | Bi | 9/7/1Bi | 9/7/1Bj |
|---|---|---|---|---|---|---|---|---|---|---|
| Anna | Joseph | John | Ann | Charles | Maria | Mary | Frederick Samuel LINDOP | Barbara DENSON | William | Francis |

Bh
Frederick Samuel
LINDOP
(1848>
848389

=
1875

Bi
Barbara
DENSON
(1848-1880>
848/103

| Ca | Cb | Cc | Cd | Ce | Cf |
|---|---|---|---|---|---|
| Frederick Samuel LINDOP (1879> 879415 | Elenor (Nellie) LINDOP 87M416 | Philis Mabel LINDOP 87M418 | Frances Muriel (Bernie) LINDOP 87M420 | Thomas Cawley WORRELL 87M421 | Bertha Dorothy (Dolly) LINDOP 87M422 |
| | She married George MULLOCK | She married Harold GORDON | = | | |

Cd = Ce:
Frances Muriel (Bernie) LINDOP = Thomas Cawley WORRELL

Thomas farmed at Mill Farm, Bumper Lane, Chester with his
wife Bernie and her sister Dolly.

Da
Frederick Samuel
(Derek) LINDOP

Ea
Frederick Samuel
LINDOP

Eb
Barbara LINDOP

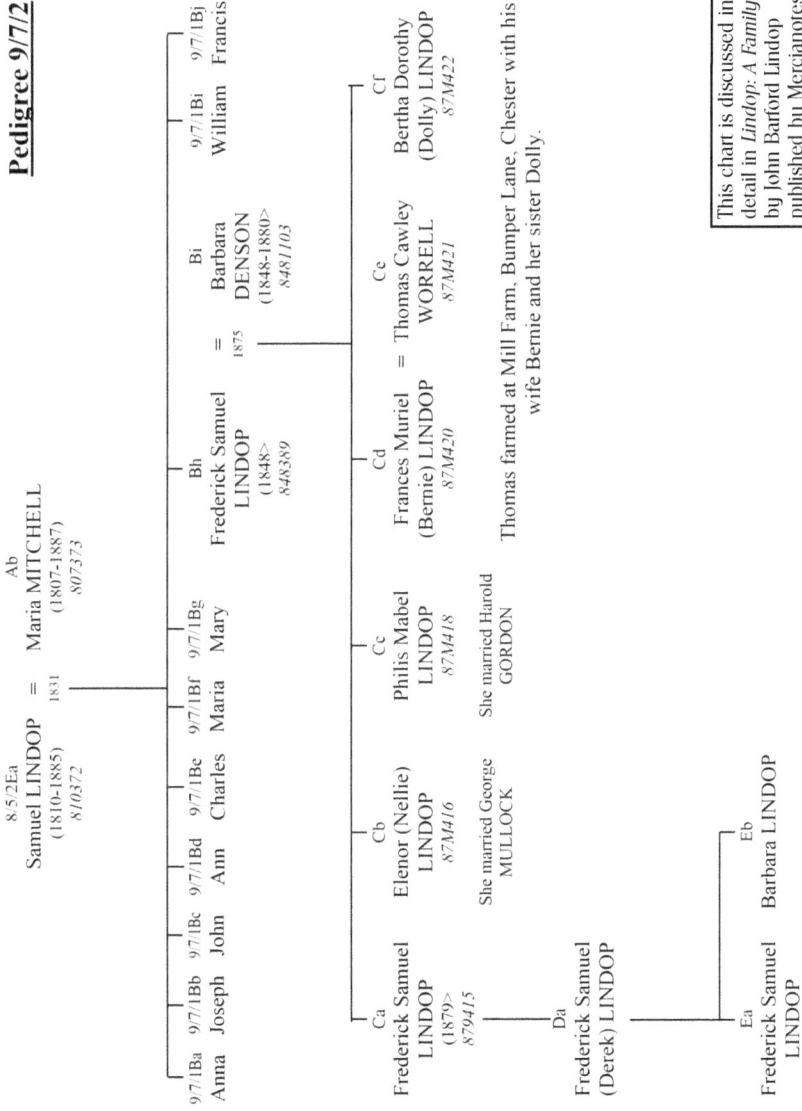

This chart is discussed in more
detail in *Lindop: A Family History*
by John Barford Lindop
published by Mercianotes.
(ISBN: 9781522882947 )

# Pedigree 9/7/3

8/5/2Ea
Samuel LINDOP  =  Maria MITCHELL
(1810-1885)    1831    (1807-1887)
810372                807373

| 9/7/1Ba | 9/7/1Bb | 9/7/1Bc | 9/7/1Bd | 9/7/1Be | 9/7/1Bf | 9/7/1Bg | 9/7/1Bh | Bi | Bj | 9/7/1Bj |
|---|---|---|---|---|---|---|---|---|---|---|
| Anna | Joseph | John | Ann | Charles | Maria | Mary | Frederick | William Edward LINDOP | = Mary Elizabeth TINKER | Francis |

William Edward LINDOP = Mary Elizabeth TINKER  1884

| Ca | Cb | Cc | Cd | Ce | Cf | Cg | Ch | Ci | Cj |
|---|---|---|---|---|---|---|---|---|---|
| Mabel LINDOP (1887>) 887397 | Frances LINDOP (1889) 889398 | William Alfred LINDOP (1890-1996) 890399 | Emily LINDOP (1850>) | Frederick Deakin LINDOP (1892>) | Earnest Charles LINDOP (1893-1918) | Dorothy LINDOP (1895>) | Nora LINDOP (1897>) | Marjorie LINDOP (1899>) | Horace Tinker LINDOP (1902-1964) |
| Married into the WHALEY family | | Married Sibley Barford WORRAL and had three children, one being John Barford LINDOP the family historian | Married into the BAKER family | | emigrated to USA in 1912 and was killed in action five weeks before the end of the First World War. | Married into the MOULDING family | Married into the WILCOX family. | Married into the EVANS family. | |

This chart is discussed in more detail in *Lindop: A Family History* by John Barford Lindop published by Mercianotes. (ISBN: 9781522882947 )

# Pedigree 9/8/1

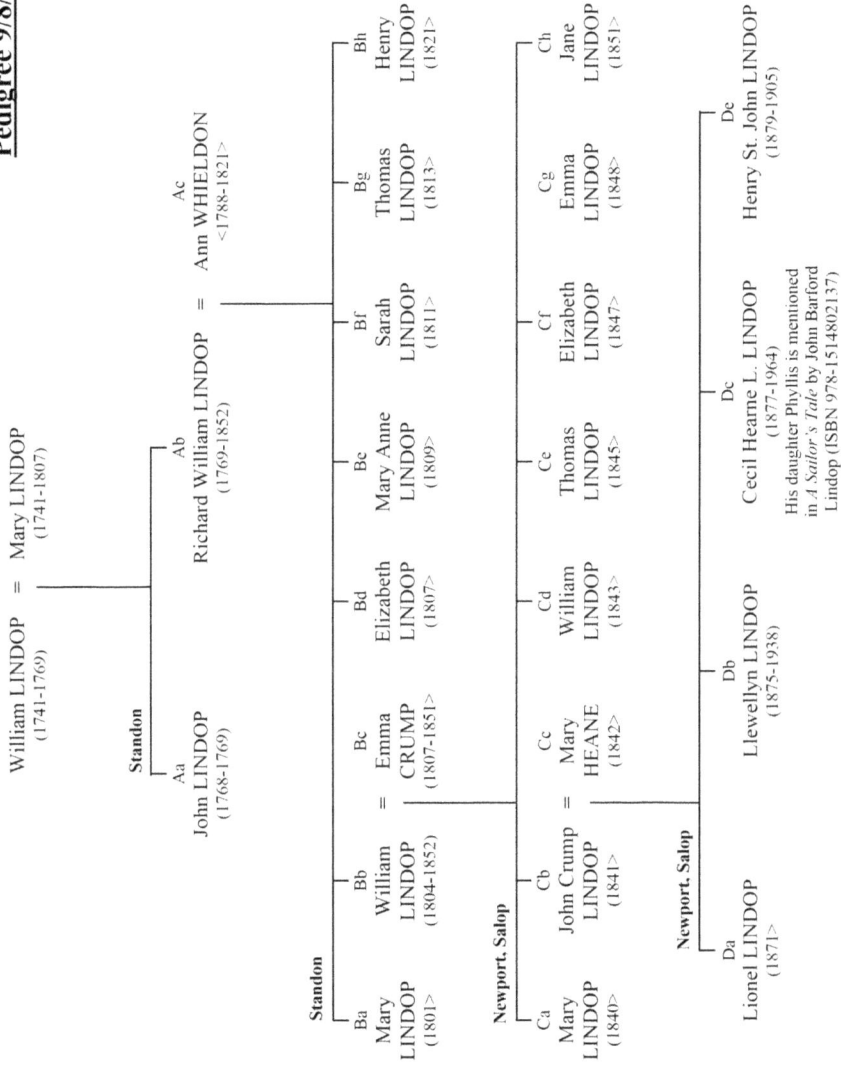

William LINDOP
(1741-1769)
=
Mary LINDOP
(1741-1807)

**Standon**

Aa
John LINDOP
(1768-1769)

Ab
Richard William LINDOP
(1769-1852)
=
Ac
Ann WHIELDON
<1788-1821>

**Standon**

Ba
Mary
LINDOP
(1801>

Bb
William
LINDOP
(1804-1852)
=
Bc
Emma
CRUMP
(1807-1851>

Bd
Elizabeth
LINDOP
(1807>

Be
Mary Anne
LINDOP
(1809>

Bf
Sarah
LINDOP
(1811>

Bg
Thomas
LINDOP
(1813>

Bh
Henry
LINDOP
(1821>

**Newport, Salop**

Ca
Mary
LINDOP
(1840>

Cb
John Crump
LINDOP
(1841>
=
Cc
Mary
HEANE
(1842>

Cd
William
LINDOP
(1843>

Ce
Thomas
LINDOP
(1845>

Cf
Elizabeth
LINDOP
(1847>

Cg
Emma
LINDOP
(1848>

Ch
Jane
LINDOP
(1851>

**Newport, Salop**

Da
Lionel LINDOP
(1871>

Db
Llewellyn LINDOP
(1875-1938)

Dc
Cecil Hearne L. LINDOP
(1877-1964)

His daughter Phyllis is mentioned
in *A Sailor's Tale* by John Barford
Lindop (ISBN 978-1514802137)

De
Henry St. John LINDOP
(1879-1905)

**Pedigree 9/9/1**

Aa
John MAINWARING
(1796-1836+)

=

Ab
Mary

Ba
Elizabeth
MAINWARING
(1826-1905)
*826462*

=

8/5/2Dd
John
LINDOP
(1816-1895)
*816376*

8/5/2Db
Samuel LINDOP
(1776-1842)
*777104*
*777365*

=

8/5/2Dc
Mary EVANS
(1784-1842)
*784145*

Bl
Peter
MITCHELL

=

8/5/2Eg
Margaret
LINDOP
(1821-1850>
*821379*

8/5/2Ea
Samuel

8/5/2Eb
William

8/5/2Ec
Thomas

8/5/2Ec
Mary

8/5/2Ef
Richard

8/5/2Eh
Joseph

8/5/2Ei
Mary Ann

8/5/2Ej
Edwin

Cc
Mary Lindop MITCHELL
(1850-1891>
*850/086*

Cb
Jane LAWRENCE
(1852-1886)
*852428*

=
1874

Cb
Joshua John LINDOP
(1850-1891>
*850427*

=
1887

Da
Alma
LINDOP
(1876>
*876433*

Db
Archibald
LINDOP
(1878>
*878434*

Dc
John
LINDOP
(1879>
*879435*

Dd
Maud
LINDOP
(1881>
*881436*

De
Oscar Sandford
LINDOP
(1889-1924)
*889/087*

Df
Dora Margaret
LINDOP
(1891-1901>
*891437*

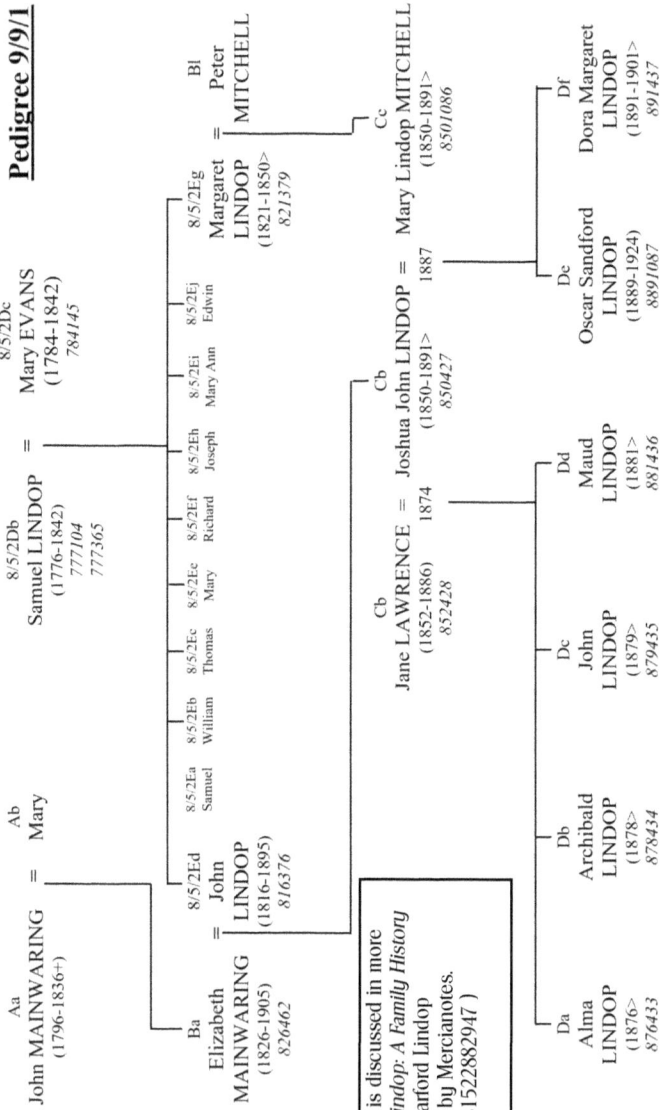

This chart is discussed in more
detail in *Lindop: A Family History*
by John Barford Lindop
published by Mercianotes.
(ISBN: 9781522882947 )

www.ingramcontent.com/pod-product-compliance
Lightning Source LLC
Chambersburg PA
CBHW052201090426
42741CB00010B/2362